Decorative Painting
For Children's Rooms

Decorative Painting
For Children's Rooms

ROSIE FISHER

with Jane Laing

NORTH LIGHT BOOKS

Cincinnati, Ohio

For Giles, Lucinda, Rupert and Tara with my love

First published in Great Britain in 1989
by Macdonald & Co (Publishers) Ltd
London & Sydney

First published in the United States 1990
by North Light Books,
an imprint of F&W Publications,
1507 Dana Avenue,
Cincinnati, Ohio 45207

ISBN 0−89134−321−0

Printed and bound in Italy by Graphicom

Editor: Jennifer Jones
Senior Art Editor: Bobbie Colgate-Stone
Designer: Sheila Volpe
Photographer: John Hollingshead
Indexer: Alexandra Corrin

CONTENTS

*I*NTRODUCTION

There can be fewer greater pleasures in life, especially for a mother, than planning a room for your child, particularly if it's for your first baby. A whole new world is suddenly upon you and although you will be over the moon with excitement, you may also feel a little lost and wonder where you should start, what you will need and what safety angles should be considered. Being a mother of four children – Giles, Lucinda, Rupert and Tara – I have learnt so much (and am still learning) and I often look back and wonder how Giles survived as I knew so little at the tender age of nineteen! There are no A Levels in motherhood, it is meant to come naturally, but you do need help and guidance and often a book can give you that.

In *Decorating Children's Rooms* I have tried to give you lots of ideas from which to choose, based on ten years' experience of running Dragons of Walton Street, which specializes in hand-painted furniture and interior design for children. We have had great fun helping to plan the rooms for our clients' children (indeed, many of our best ideas have come from clients' suggestions) and the results can be seen throughout this book.

You do not have to be a great artist to try out the ideas shown here either! You could try just a paint finish, a simple sponge, a wash or drag. Then, when you have mastered that, you could add a few simple flowers and bows or one or two of your child's favourite storybook characters. Children are much easier to please and one day will really appreciate your having painted something especially for them!

Previous pages, right and opposite: with her exceptional skill and eye for detail, Elli Yannis has created a magnificent Dragons' dolls' house featuring miniature versions of our hand-painted furniture.

Painting on fabric is another area you might like to explore: ideas for decorating bed linen, curtains and blinds are all given in this book. Throughout you will find ideas for painting murals, from relatively simple efforts to quite complicated schemes. In each chapter you'll also find a practical, stage-by-stage room project showing how to achieve a number of decorative effects, and at the end of the book there are detailed instructions on how to create the many paint techniques illustrated in the book. Essentials such as basic furniture, fittings and safety are also discussed in detail, to help you plan ahead to the next age group.

There is so much scope today with many more wallpapers, fabrics and furniture especially designed for children available on the market. Decorating your child's room is such a fulfilling project, so do not rush into it, take your time, choose carefully and enjoy it all – they're only children for such a short time!

Rosie Fisher.

BABIES 0–2

One of the main considerations in decorating your baby's room is to create both a practical and a pleasing environment for you and your child. The emphasis in this book is on decorative treatments, but practical and safety matters are particularly important when planning bedrooms for small babies and toddlers. So before you start thinking about the décor, look at the room from a practical point of view, especially if this is going to be your child's room for some years to come. Once you have examined the basic requirements of the room, which are looked at in detail at the end of this chapter (see pages 30–3), the decorative side can come to the fore.

The first part of this chapter looks at general schemes using a number of decorative treatments, and is followed by the main theme of the chapter, stencilling. An easy technique to master, you can make your designs as simple or as complicated as you like, from straightforward borders made up, for example, of squares and diamonds in various complementary colours, to stencilled motifs of animals, clowns, balloons, rainbows and kites.

Whatever you have in mind, take a tip from interior designers and prepare a sample board before you start. Pin all the samples you have collected—a square of carpet, a swatch of curtain fabric, a paint chip—on to cardboard, and take a good look at how all the colours, patterns and textures work together (you may like to make up two or three variations); this will also give you an idea of the overall effect of the final scheme. Leave your sample board in the room and look at it at different times of the day to assess how the colours compare in daylight and artificial light. Take your time at this stage, and give yourself the opportunity to play around with the samples you have collected until you are satisfied that you have found the right combination.

DECORATING IDEAS

Before you decide on all the decorative details for your baby's room, think carefully about the overall colour scheme in relation to the room's size and aspect. Is it a large, rectangular room with a big window on the south side of the building, receiving sun for most of the day? Or is it a small, awkwardly shaped room with a tiny window that faces north, receiving very little sun? A room that is flooded with light for most of the day will be able to take the cooler colours, such as blues, blue-greens and turquoises, without seeming cold. But a large, dark room will need some warm, sunny colours to cheer it up, such as reds, oranges, yellows, beiges,

creams and apricots. Babies thrive in a reassuring atmosphere that is also stimulating, and, on the whole, people find that pastel colours are easier on the eye, and therefore more relaxing, than bright primaries or stronger shades. So, you could either paint the walls in a solid colour, or you might consider sponging them (see page 142) in two shades of one pastel colour to give a soft, delicate finish. You could then extend this approach to the furniture you have in the room—such as the nursing chair, chest of drawers and cot—uniting all the elements and providing a good base for repeating motifs or pat-

Page 10: in this charming interior, the warm mellow tones of antique pine wall panelling are complemented by the subtle sheen of off-white, satin lacquered furniture and an elegant silk *crêpe baldachino* at the head of the cot. They are combined with cuddly soft toys, and coordinated pastel coloured cot stencils and curtain fabric, to create a warm, bright bedroom.

Right: inspired by the garden beyond, pastel green, pale yellow and earthy-brown coloured soft furnishings are employed to complement the mellow tones of antique pine and wickerwork furniture, while off-white walls and a large mirror reflect the abundance of natural light, to accentuate the sense of spaciousness.

terns. Make sure, however, that the paint you use is non-toxic and lead-free (see page 133) on any surfaces that your baby is likely to chew on later.

Changing the shape of the room

If the room is large, use warm colours, even on the ceiling, to help make the room seem smaller. To bring the ceiling down even further, paint it in a darker tone or shade to the wall colour. If the ceiling is very high, continue the darker colour right down to picture-rail level. Another way to effectively reduce the size of a room is to divide it with a pretty screen or curtain,

and place the pieces of furniture strategically around the room, creating interesting angles and focal points.

If the room is very small, keep furniture to a minimum (a trolley that you can tuck into a corner when you are not using it will be useful here) so that you and the baby have some floor space, and use cooler colours, such as soft, pale greens and blues on walls, ceilings and fabrics.

Patterns have varying visual effects too: choose a pale, small-patterned (wipeable) wallpaper if you want the room to appear larger, and one with a large design if you wish the room to seem smaller.

Above: whilst large patterns normally make a room seem smaller, here the predominant elephant motif blends the coordinated soft furnishings and furniture into the surrounding walls – an effect which actually increases the visual sense of space. At the same time, the striking combination of lilac, pink and green coloured elephants set against a bright yellow background establishes a feeling of warmth and fun.

Right: this detail reveals how muted pastel colours (in the rug) can provide an effective backcloth to the brighter, more vivid colours often used in children's toys.

Below: plain, biscuit coloured walls complement the stained and polished wooden floorboards and skirting, echo a predominant colour in the rug and provide a light, warm and understated backdrop for the cot and bedding. Such a simple, unfussy décor prevents any feeling of clutter.

Coordinating colours

It is visually easiest, when working up a colour scheme, to start with your main background wall colour first; choose one that, amongst other things, suits the aspect and proportions of the room, as discussed in the preceding paragraphs. For a well-balanced, blended scheme, select colours for the rest of the room that are closely related to your main wall colour. For example, with pale pink walls try introducing shades of deep apricot, soft raspberry and even peach to decorative borders, curtains, carpets and bedlinen. These colours, which also vary in intensity—i.e. from light through to mid and dark tones—will provide your scheme with depth and

lightness. You can, of course, work up a scheme that is based on tones of only one colour, from its lightest tint to its darkest shade, but in both cases your schemes will benefit from the introduction of a few 'accent' colours. These are colours that obviously contrast with your main colour scheme, such as a light colour set against predominantly darker ones, or a splash of cool colour against mainly warm colours. Also, use complementary colours to brighten up your scheme; for example, in the pink scheme described above, you might choose a curtain fabric that includes light green in the design, or introduce some green into the decorative border. Used sparingly, accents and complementaries will add life and interest to your scheme.

Link-in the pieces of furniture too, by painting them in the same colour and style as the walls for a really coordinated effect; or paint them plain eggshell white for a fresh, practical surface on which to decorate with stencilled motifs.

Once you have painted the furniture why not try copying a friendly looking animal, such as a kitten or a rabbit, taken from a book or magazine, and trace it several times on to each of the drawers of a chest, to make a symmetrical pattern. You can then trace the same character or set of characters on to the other pieces of furniture, including the cot, before painting them carefully one colour at a time. Try painting the same motifs on the blinds or curtains, the duvet cover or coverlet, cot bumpers, and on smaller items such as a clock or small wooden lamp stand. (You could also use these motifs on wall surfaces—either freehand or stencilled.) You will need to scale the motif (or motifs) up or down, according to the size of the area you wish to fill. The traditional method of squaring up is described on page 150, or use a photocopier that can reduce or enlarge your drawing to the correct scale.

Camouflaging fixtures and fittings

If you have fitted cupboards that you want to play down, you could continue the paint effect used on the walls, so that they merge into the background. This will create a cohesive look that will make the room seem larger still. If the cupboards are attractive, say with panelled doors or interesting mouldings, paint them in a lighter or deeper tone than the wall colour, so that they stand out in contrast.

Alternatively, use the same paint effect on the cupboards as that used on the walls, but draw attention to any interesting features. For example, if you have painted the walls a pale turquoise, extend this to the cupboards, and then accentuate the mouldings and handles by picking them out with a slightly darker shade of turquoise. If the cupboards are completely flat, you could

Above: the rabbits and balloons embellishing this white lacquered cot were stencilled in soft pastel blue, peach and pink colours to echo the floor rugs and picture frames; whilst closer inspection reveals a matching pink ribbon around the carry cot. Employing the same or similar colours over different objects and surfaces pulls them together into a cohesive decorative scheme.

Above: this charming attic bedroom has a four-poster cot and matching toybox, table and chairs, all embellished with pastel coloured rabbit stencils and coordinated fabric, to complete the fairytale theme.

Opposite page: pastel pinks, blues and yellows are employed to embellish door and drawer mouldings, co-ordinate different surfaces and stencil the teddy bear theme in this baby's bedroom.

give them the same finish as used on the walls, and then paint a mural over both to disguise the cupboards and introduce an exciting feature into the room. This can be very effective, and an excellent way of camouflaging or playing down an unwanted fixture. However, you will have to think hard as to whether it is really worth painting a complex mural—your child is likely to outgrow the subject and style within a few years. But, if you paint the mural in soft, pastel colours it will be easier to cover up later on. Another idea is to paint a basic sky and grass mural and stick removable characters on top that can be taken down and changed as your child's interests develop.

Radiators can present a similar problem

to ugly cupboards. Either camouflage them with the same paint treatment as on the walls, or be daring and draw attention to them by painting them in a bright contrasting colour, or a multi-coloured spatter finish (see page 145).

Introducing a sense of fun

If the room is awkwardly shaped with an immovable fixture, such as a low beam, why not make the most of both features? For example, highlight any beams by painting them in a deeper shade than the wall colour, and make them the starting point for a decorative 'theme' for the rest of the room: paint more *trompe-l'oeil* beams around the room, where they might well naturally appear, and add little friendly creatures, such as mice, rabbits or kittens, dancing along them. If you have decided on mice as a theme, you could paint one or two mouseholes on the skirting board, and have the mice darting in and out of them.

The room may contain a fireplace, long ago bricked up. If it is truly ugly, you could knock it out completely and create a useful space for storing toys. But if it is fairly presentable, and you are planning to paint a mural, why not make it the focal point: transform it into an unusual-looking house, perhaps part of a whole street; or paint a glorious fire burning in the grate with a friendly looking dog or cat lying asleep in front of it (such a scene could always be painted on to a small screen and placed in front of the actual fireplace).

If you do not feel up to painting murals or *trompe l'oeil*, try adding pattern by stencilling. Make your own or buy ready-made ones, which can then be used to stencil designs on virtually any surface, as long as you use the right paint for the surface you are painting (see paint guide, pages 132–4). It is an ideal method of producing a simple repeating design for borders and accentuating the shape of a room.

MURALS

Murals do not necessarily have to be complex scenes painted all around the room. You could paint just one character with a small amount of background on to a portion of one wall, to create a very eye-catching image. For a baby's room, try recreating characters from nursery rhymes or fairy tales. Trace the characters from a book and scale up the drawings (see page 150) to fit the space. Then paint the image one colour at a time.

Another effective idea for a small mural would be to paint a cat to one side of the window, either sitting with his back to you

peering outside or poised about to leap through it. A small row of teddy bears, rabbits or balloons painted on the bottom corner of one wall would add a small, amusing feature to a baby's room.

If you have stencilled a particular animal or character around your baby's room, why not try to incorporate the same animal in its setting in a mural: a hippo half-submerged in water, a cat asleep in his basket, rabbits walking along a farm track. Start with a simple shape and a little background and gradually expand the scenario as you grow more confident.

Above: the cot is decorated with an attention-grabbing yellow teddy, and balloons to match those on the wall.

Right: traced and coloured balloons and clowns provide a focal point for a resting baby.

Opposite page: variations on a theme provide motifs for the walls, toybox and children's furniture in this charming nursery.

STENCILLING IDEAS

Simple, stencilled motifs and characters are just right for a baby's room, providing colourful, interesting shapes that will catch your baby's attention. By stencilling the motifs, rather than drawing and painting them freehand, you will find it much easier to produce a row of shapes that match exactly, and the task of decorating a whole room will seem far less arduous.

Use the same core of motifs throughout the room—as a decorative frieze on walls, floors, furniture and fabrics. This will help you to create a completely coordinated look. By using small motifs, painting them in pastel colours, and applying them discreetly only on selected surfaces, you will have a scheme that is both attractive and easy to create.

A stencilled design can be used to 'alter' the shape of the room too. If it has a high ceiling, introduce a line where the dado rail would be by stencilling a line of, say, ducks or trees all the way around the room (see also pages 24–9). This will provide a cheerful decorative effect and make the room appear smaller. You could use a different paint technique or put up a different wallpaper below this border, to complete the effect. To reduce visually the height of the room further, repeat the motif, or stencil a different one, in an attractive border higher up the wall, at, for example, picture-rail level.

A simple stencilled border

Plan your design carefully before buying or cutting the stencils you have in mind. It is probably best to start with really easy shapes if you have not tried stencilling before: squares and circles, for example, are good basic shapes which can be turned into simple but effective designs. Try out various colour combinations with different sizes and combinations of shapes on strips of card. Then stick them on to the surface to be decorated (using low-tack masking tape, which shouldn't pull the paint away when you remove it). Place the card at the point where you want the border to be, then stand back so that you can assess which size, shape and colour works best.

If the wall is painted in a colour other than white, try out the stencil shapes on card painted in the same colour and paint technique as that used on the wall, because the background colour will affect the top colour. For example, mid-blue painted on yellow will take on a slightly green tinge, while mid-blue painted on pink will look slightly mauve.

Once you have decided on, say, a low border of alternating pastel blue diamonds and pastel yellow or orange circles, and have determined their sizes, mark off the base line of the border all the way around the room to ensure that the line of shapes does not waver. Rule off the vertical line,

Below: this teddy bears' picnic wall stencil presents a colourful, happy scene sure to grab the attention of young eyes. Note how light dabbing (pouncing) with the stencil brush has created areas of light and shade across the surface of the balloons and honey jar, giving them a simple, three-dimensional quality of form.

too, as a guide for the first stencil if it is a more complicated design. Line up each shape carefully against the previous one to ensure that the row does not lean forwards or backwards, or both (see pages 24–9). Proceed by stencilling all the blue diamonds first and then go back to the beginning and fill in the spaces with the yellow or orange circles.

Linking and defining borders
You may want to create another stencilled border on the wall, perhaps at the top. This should link with the first border in terms of style, content and colour, so that together they provide a cohesive framework around the room. They need not be exactly the same, however. Try using different geometric shapes or altering one of the colours.

Above: stencilled teddies, balloons and trees lend visual interest to otherwise plain walls. The lampshade, cupboard and chair cushion are similarly decorated; whilst the repeat tree stencil above the picture rail emphasises the proportions of the room.

Right: drawing on the kite for inspiration, the walls, floorboards, ceiling and door panels of this fascinating bedroom have been decorated with a cloudy sky mural and then embellished with brightly coloured stencilled kites, clouds and rainbows. The slightly cool cast of the predominant pale blue is balanced by the mellow warmth of the polished pine.

To further define both borders, rule off a thin line at the top and bottom of the motifs and paint them in a slightly darker shade of one of the colours used in the shapes. Use low-tack masking tape on either side of the rules, so that you paint clean lines. This simple addition will prevent the geometric shapes from appearing to 'float' on the wall, while fixing them in position and drawing attention to them.

Character themes

For a more adventurous border, try buying or cutting stencils of plants, animals or friendly looking characters, such as teddy bears or clowns. For a simple but charming effect, the bears could all link arms as they do when cut as a long line from a piece of folded paper. Or stencil individual figures, or alternate between, say, bears and rocking-horses. Cartoon-style elephants or hippopotami could stroll along a low border, while seagulls or balloons might fly along a high border. Try the alternate shapes idea to create simple scenes: stencil a frog about to leap over a waterlily all the way around the room, or a dog chasing a ball, or a cat chasing a mouse.

Think also of other surfaces in the room while creating a border. Other parts of the wall could be stencilled with a group of bears or clowns doing different things. You do not need to stencil exactly the same design on to the furniture and fabrics, but it is a good idea to retain the same theme and use the same colours. So, for example, if a cat chasing a mouse makes up the wall border, try stencilling cats and mice occupied differently and separately on, say, the cot. Or paint smaller details of a stencil on, say, a chair or a small chest of drawers. A cat might simply be sitting in a basket, or sharpening his claws against the cot legs, or cat after cat might be running down the cot legs, or across the cot head. A mouse might be licking its whiskers or sniffing the air, or peering at a mousetrap, or once again, mouse after mouse might be running down the legs of the cot.

Stencilling fabric

Elephants or hippopotami might seem rather cumbersome subjects for curtains or blinds, but if you use them on a small scale and in the same colours as elsewhere in the room they can look surprisingly 'right'. Stencil the repeating pattern downwards, drawing vertical keylines before applying the stencil and paint. If you have already chosen elephants and hippos for the walls, you might like to try a column of trumpeting elephants—quite widely spaced—followed by a column of hippos, face on. Stagger the columns, so that each animal is surrounded by space. Take care to keep the columns straight and not to smudge the preceding character when you are laying down the

next stencil—wait until it is dry before continuing, or space the characters farther apart.

You could also stencil a character or characters on the duvet cover and bumpers in the cot. For a change, try creating a large single stencilled character, but choose one that still relates to the characters stencilled in other places in the room. Try a sleeping cat, or a wallowing hippo, for instance. Then stencil smaller running mice or walking elephants around the edge to frame the central image. When painting the stencil, slip a piece of card between the layers of the duvet cover to prevent the paint coming through on to the lower layer.

Combining stencils

You can often combine small and large stencilled motifs by using a large image framed by smaller ones, say, on a wardrobe or on a door with panels. Larger images, of course, are more likely to require several stencils and several colours; so do not attempt them until you have mastered the art of applying the simpler motifs. When you feel up to coping with something more complex, try a peacock with all its feathers spread out like a fan. This would look beautiful set in the centres of two adjacent panels, framed, either by lining the panels or by stencilling a border of small peacocks. More simply, a stylized tree with buds would look very effective.

Even if you decide on such complicated panels, you could still do a simple border at the top and bottom of the wardrobe, perhaps a whole row of stylized trees, walking birds, or balloons. Three or four balloons in different shades, and tied together with string, would look very effective repeated far apart, floating down the side of the wardrobe, or falling from top to bottom of the blinds or curtains. Try stencilling a teddy bear holding on to the end of the string, to complete the motif.

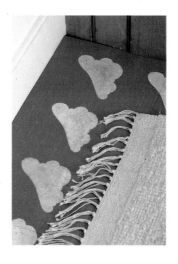

Above: these floorboards have been colourwashed in a pastel mauve-blue (see page 147); decorated with a repeat stencilled cloud motif, which has been lightly sponged in white and very pale blue (see page 142), and finally varnished for protection. Decorating the perimeter of a floor in this manner, combining it with loose-lay rugs, and coordinating it with other surfaces in the room, can provide a cheaper, and more attractive alternative to the usual fitted carpets.

Below left: the loose-fit cushion of this elegant white cane and wicker armchair has been tastefully decorated with brightly coloured balloon stencils (which match the décor elsewhere in the room). This is a particularly good example of how stencils, applied with discretion, can be used to make plain, 'adult' furniture more fun for children.

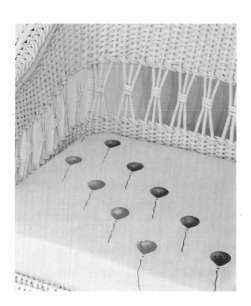

PROJECT ONE
A STENCILLED ROOM

The bright, yet gentle atmosphere of this small attic nursery is largely due to the choice of off-white and yellows chosen for the decorative scheme. The simple duck motifs stencilled in bright yellow on the walls, on the toybox, and on the blue lampshade impart a fresh and slightly humorous accent to the room. Variety in the stencilled scheme is introduced by the slightly different poses of the ducks and ducklings, apart from the basic ones of walking and swimming. There is even an odd one out – the ugly duckling – which is painted a different colour on the toybox.

The stylized grass motif on the wall provides a delicate pattern that supports the frieze of ducks walking around the room, and the positioning of single ducklings waddling and paddling among it helps to tie it in with the frieze above. The stencilling is all the more effective because it is not overwhelming: ducks have not been stencilled on absolutely every available surface; in fact, much of the room is quite plain. The scheme is cohesive without being tediously repetitive, yet clearly draws together the disparate parts of the room.

When making such a stencilled frieze around a room, it is important to ensure that your stencilled motifs are not going up- or downhill, or the effect will be most alarming. Decide on the height of the frieze, and mark this point off on the wall. Then, using a spirit level, a ruler, and soft-lead pencil or chalk, rule off the horizontal base of the frieze (as shown in photograph 1 on page 26. It is best to use a spirit level rather than measuring up or down at

1. Rule the top line of the dado area with a soft-lead pencil and ruler. When painting borders or friezes, it is important to have a perfectly straight, horizontal guideline.

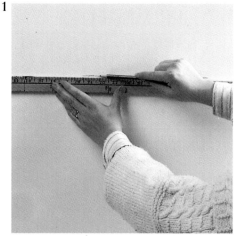

2. Mark the positions of the repeating motifs, ensuring that they are an equal distance apart. Fix the stencil to the wall with low-tack masking tape.

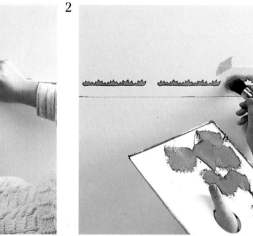

3. Carefully line up the feature motifs. Paint one colour at a time, dabbing, or pouncing, from the outside edges towards the centres. Do not overload the brush.

4. Rule up a grid for a dado area to ensure that the repeating pattern of small motifs lines up perfectly.

5. Position the small grass motifs at the crossover points of the grid and fix to the wall with masking tape. Add details, such as the eyes of the ducks, last, for that expressive finishing touch.

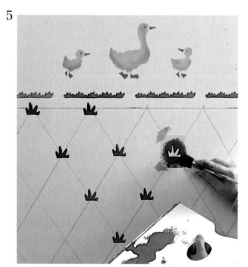

intervals from the floor or ceiling as either may be out of true, resulting in the creation of an uneven line.

Next, mark the position of the first motif that will be depicted above this line (in this case, stylized grass). At this point, a parallel line was ruled above the first to introduce some space between the solid line of grass motifs and the ducks above. Place the stencil in position and fix it in place with low-tack masking tape. Mix up your first colour and place it in a saucer. Make sure that you mix enough to fill in all the areas that call for this colour, as you might have difficulty matching the colour

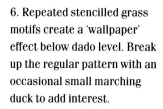

6. Repeated stencilled grass motifs create a 'wallpaper' effect below dado level. Break up the regular pattern with an occasional small marching duck to add interest.

later. Although expensive, artists' acrylic paints are most appropriate for stencilling as they dry quickly, allowing the speedy imposition of one stencil on another after the first has been painted. To minimize the cost, mix artists' acrylic colour with white emulsion to create a pastel shade. Dip the stencil brush in the paint and dab away the excess on a spare piece of paper: the brush tips should almost be dry. With a dabbing, or pouncing, action, fill in the stencil, starting from the outsides and working towards the centre (as shown in photograph 2).

When stencilling you should always work with one colour at a time, finishing one before starting with another. So, in this case, the grass motifs should be completed before returning to the starting point and stencilling the first group of ducks between the grass motifs. After deciding on the exact position of the first grouping and fixing the duck stencils in place with low-tack masking tape, the ducks should be stencilled one colour at a time. First, the main part of each body is dabbed with chrome yellow, taking care to avoid adjacent cut-outs. To make the body appear curvaceous, when the yellow paint is dry, mix a little vermilion with the chrome yellow and dab around the body curves. Then, using a different brush, the orange-red beaks and feet can be painted (as shown in photograph 3).

After completing the frieze, it is a good idea to draw a grid up to facilitate the accurate painting of a regularly patterned area beneath the frieze, such as the grass motif shown here. Divide it into diamond shapes by measuring off equal distances along the top and bottom of the area, using a soft pencil and a metre rule. Here, a top

7. Try painting white or yellow ducks on dark backgrounds, as on this navy blue lampshade. It is always a good idea to stencil coordinating accessories, as this gives your child's room a real 'designer' look.

point was matched to a bottom point three points to the left and to another three points to the right (as shown in photograph 4 on page 26). this was then repeated all the way along. The grass stencil was then placed at the centre point where each line crosses to create the diagonal pattern.

When the yellow paint is absolutely dry, the finishing touch can be given to the stencilled ducks by painting beady black eyes on each with a fine sable brush. Alternatively, you could use a black felt-tip pen. After this, the small grass motif is positioned and painted at each crossover point on the grid (as shown in photograph 5 on page 26). A few spaces are left in which solitary ducks can be stencilled in later, to introduce a little variety.

When the dado is completed, the wall above it can be embellished with small groupings of stencilled ducks. In the room shown on page 24, a touch of humour was incorporated by positioning the ducks within each group in an interesting and amusing way. Any mistakes were rectified by waiting for the acrylic paint to dry, and then touching the unwanted paint out with the base-colour emulsion. Small slips were left untouched, however, as slight inconsistencies were thought to add charm to the overall stencilled pattern of the room.

It is interesting to note that stencils need not be used in a static way. Here, each grouping of ducks and ducklings – wherever they are used – tells a story because the ducks relate to one another. In the frieze, for example, one duck appears to be talking to a duckling, who is not listening but looking forward to another duckling; one duck has turned away from his neighbour;

another duckling is apparently gazing up at his parent for reassurance. Further up the wall, one grouping depicts several ducklings swimming hither and thither around a parent duck, the wave stencils used to indicate movement through water. In another group on the wall, all the ducklings are paddling obediently in the same direction but one lags a long way behind the others. Compose your groups carefully, so that they make interesting studies. Try out different ideas on rough paper until you are happy with the colours and arrangements you have designed.

If you do not feel up to stencilling an entire wall, try stencilling a simple frieze of waddling ducks around a lampshade to make a pretty accessory. Or stencil groups of ducks and borders on to a toybox to make it more lively and fun to look at. On the toybox in this nursery, clumps of grass were stencilled in a border around the top to frame a group of one duck and two ducklings, this time painted in white against the primrose yellow base colour. Each end of the toybox was also embellished with ducks, in chrome yellow and orange. On one side of the toybox, a trail of parent duck and three ducklings was depicted paddling through marshland. The scene was made more poignant by painting the last duckling – separated from the others by a clump of grass – deep blue; obviously he is the spurned ugly duckling.

8. A toybox can be fun to paint if you do not feel sufficiently confident to tackle a whole wall or room.

BABIES: Basic Room

Throughout the book, in each basic requirements section, you will find an up-dated version of the room illustrated below. The idea is to show how, in principle, the same room can be changed around to cater for all the different age groups, with the minimum of expense and effort. Here, a built-in cupboard and shelves have been installed and a large chest of drawers placed conveniently between the two. This is used as a solid, flat surface for changing the baby,

and all the equipment is to hand on the shelves. The toybox under the window will play a useful role throughout the years as an ideal storage place, and later as a small table. Items that are useful now, but will disappear in later years, include the nursing chair, cot and trolley. Note the bars at the window and the child-proof cover over the electrical socket; safety is an important consideration at this stage, as well as the practical, such as heating and lighting.

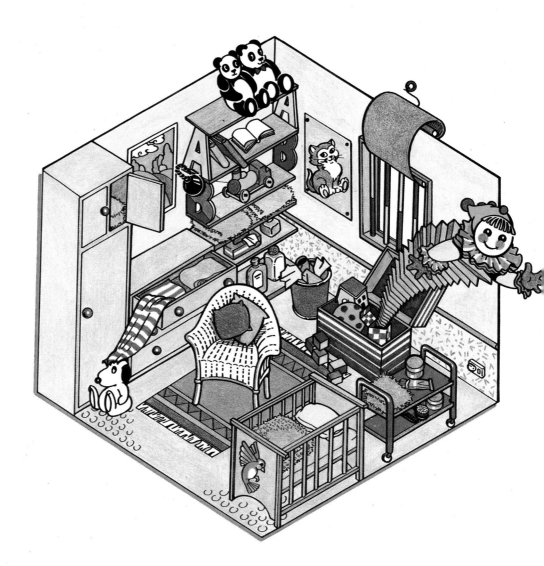

BASIC REQUIREMENTS

The furniture and décor requirements of a baby can be elaborate or simple, largely depending on the depth of your pocket. Before starting to decorate and furnish your baby's room, however, it is vital to think carefully about whether your child will still be using the room when he or she is attending school, or even when a teenager. If the room is to be for long-term use, it is a good idea to think carefully about future requirements, unless you are prepared to refurnish and redecorate every two or three years—and very few people are prepared to do this, whether for reasons of time or money. With careful planning, however, you can adjust the room to meet your child's growing needs.

Storing your baby's things

A baby does not require much storage space. A small chest of drawers will hold most of the clothes and also provide a surface for changing nappies. However, if you want to buy furniture that will last, it is a good idea to install a large chest of drawers (or two small ones) straightaway. These surfaces are perfect for nappy-changing and holding lotions and potions.

A simple wardrobe with fitted shelves will hold all the baby's clothes plus spare bedding, nappies and toys. If the room contains alcoves, you could install floor-to-ceiling cupboards in them, making the most of this area.

Sleeping arrangements

For the first few months of the baby's life, he or she will be quite happy sleeping in a cradle, carry cot or moses basket, all of which are easy to move or carry around. (Many parents find it convenient and re-assuring to have the baby sleeping in their bedroom with them.) Some small cradles are not made to any standard, so before buying, check that it is made from a harmless material and that there are no rough edges or holes in which tiny fingers could become caught. Kit it out with a firm mattress (made from combustion modified foam) with air vents and a non-airtight cover (a removable cotton mesh one is probably best).

By about four or five months (depending on how big the baby is), he or she will be ready to move into a cot. Make sure that the cot and mattress you buy are sturdy and safe, and conform to regulation standards. The materials from which the cot is made, especially the paintwork, should be non-toxic—some babies like chewing fixtures such as cot struts. If the cot is made of wood, there should be no evidence of woodworm and the surface should be absolutely smooth—no slivers to prick your baby's skin. If it is made of metal, there should be no sign of corrosion. The sides of the cot should be high enough to

Below: this baby's bedroom has been decorated with an eye to the future. Solid beech-framed storage units provide an abundance of storage space, and more can be added on at a later date, if necessary. Note in their pleasing lines the absence of any sharp edges – an important consideration when choosing furniture for babies and children.

prevent your baby from climbing out and there should be no horizontal bars for this reason. Also, the rail heights should be high enough, even when the dropside is down, to prevent the baby from falling out when asleep, and a dropside guide system should be fitted with an automatic fastening device so that the baby cannot let down the side on his or her own. In addition, the struts should not be so close together that your baby's fingers are in danger of becoming trapped, nor so wide apart that your baby's head could become caught between them. A gap of 2⅜ in (6 cm) is about right.

The mattress should be a firm safety mattress, interior sprung, or made of combustion modified foam. Make sure you buy one that is the correct size for the cot. There should be enough space around the mattress to allow the bedclothes to be tucked in (fitted cot sheets and a duvet are probably the best choice for bedding), but not enough to form a dangerous gap, and there should be no handles in which the baby's arms or legs could become trapped. The mattress should feature at least four firmly fitted ventilators in the ends or sides, and the cover of the mattress should allow the baby to breathe freely no matter which way he or she lies. A waterproof sheet should be placed on top in case of vomiting or wetting. You can get fitted waterproof sheets made from cellular

cotton, with PVC centre panels. Plastic sheets which cover the whole mattress are considered unsafe by experts.

Do not place a pillow in the cot until your baby is at least one year old, and even then your baby is probably better off without one. Buy a firm pillow that your baby's head cannot sink into, and cover it with a cotton pillowcase that fits the pillow properly. Remember to remove any protective plastic covers on mattresses and pillows.

Other furniture

If you aim to feed the baby in the room, a chair that is comfortable to sit in while you are feeding is a must: buy a firmly upholstered chair with arms and make sure that your back is firmly supported with cushions. A trolley is invaluable for keeping all the baby equipment neat and tidy and constantly within arm's reach. Blanket chests are also useful items—use them for spare bedding or for large toys later on. If there is room, it is a good idea to install a wash basin.

Lighting options

Babies are distracted by bright light, so it may be worth fitting thick roller blinds that keep out the light during long summer evenings rather than floor-length curtains that your baby can tug at.

As for artificial lighting, avoid relying on one central light that illuminates nothing well, and everything to the same extent. Instead, try fitting three spot lights in this central point, to light the room in a more interesting way and to allow a specific area, such as for nappy-changing, to be well lit, while avoiding direct light falling on your baby's eyes in the cot. Alternatively, get rid of the central light fitting entirely and fit four recessed ceiling lights towards the corners of the room, again making sure that light does not shine directly into your baby's eyes in the cot.

Below: this simple storage unit and marbled worktop makes an ideal 'work station' for changing nappies and clothing. Open cupboards and plenty of hooks on the rail behind ensure everything is immediately accessible, even with your hands full!

Heating matters

The temperature of your baby's room should be kept at an even, warm 65° to 70°F (18° to 21°C) except when you are bathing a newborn baby, when ideally the temperature should be about 80°F (27°C). So, if possible, install individually controlled radiators or electric heaters.

If you are installing central heating, fit the radiators where there is the most heat loss, for example under the window, which should be fitted with a draught excluder. In addition, it is a good idea to box in radiators so that your baby cannot scald him or herself on them. Mount electric heaters on the wall, out of the reach of your baby, and fit fireguards that comply with regulation standards to all electric, gas or paraffin heaters, or place a freestanding fireguard in front of an open fire.

Floors and walls

Short-pile carpet in mottled colours is one option for your baby's floor: warm underfoot, it will be pleasant for your baby to crawl on and will help to disguise any marks. However, when your child starts playing with modelling clay and making vegetable prints with water colours you will wish you had put down something that is easier to clean, such as cushioned vinyl, or vinyl-coated tiles.

The bottom quarter of the walls is liable to become covered with grubby finger marks or artistic scribbles in no time at all, so a major requirement for the wall finish is that it should be washable or wipeable. If you wish to hang wallpaper, then choose vinyl paper, otherwise coat an emulsion-painted finish with polyurethane varnish (but be warned, this may darken the colour of the paint), or paint with gloss paint.

Safety features

Safety is an important consideration in a baby's room. Install electrical points well out of the reach of your crawling baby's inquisitive fingers or use socket covers to prevent them from coming to any harm. Attach electrical flexes to the wall, as loose flexes are a hazard.

Make sure that all the furniture is smooth: that there are no rough edges, sharp points or protruding nails. You can buy corner protectors, which cover sharp corners on tables, shelves or units. If you are decorating the furniture, ensure that you use non-toxic, lead-free paint (see page 133). Ornaments are easily knocked over and even more easily swallowed if kept within reach of your baby, so keep them somewhere else, unless you can put them high up. Hang mobiles out of reach of your baby's hands. As soon as your baby becomes mobile you should install window locks on the inside, or vertical bars on the outside of the window (make sure that these can easily be removed in the event of an emergency). Finally, you might like to install a baby alarm system with outlets in, say, your bedroom and the lounge.

Above: again, this bright, cheerful baby's room has been furnished with future needs in mind. For now the simple units provide storage space for baby clothes and a flat surface for changing nappies. But eventually, when the cot has been changed for a bed, the units can serve as a combined wardrobe and desk. Of course, the great advantage of plenty of cupboard space is that it makes it much easier to keep the room tidy – whatever the age of the child.

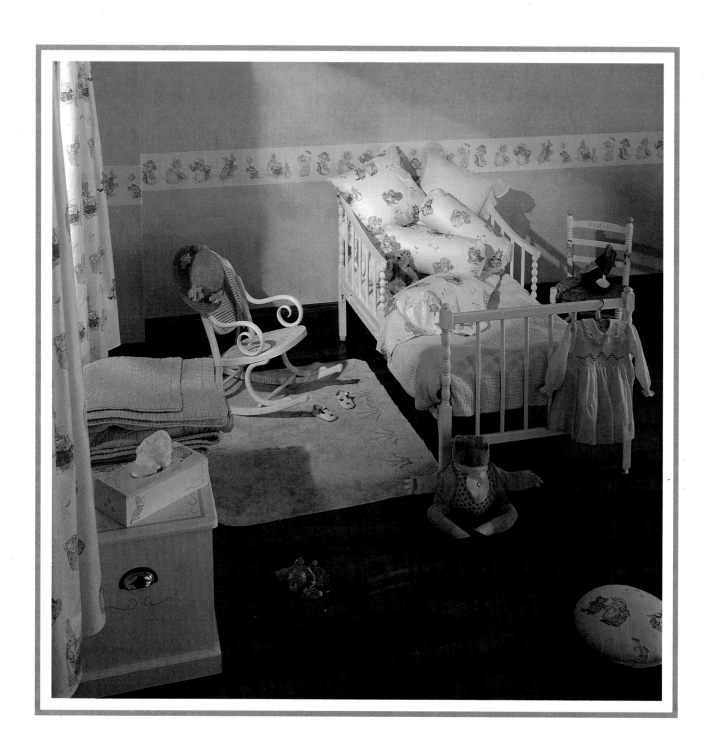

TODDLERS 2–4

The emphasis of a toddler's room is significantly different from that of a baby's. A toddler is highly inquisitive and very active, possessing a seemingly insatiable desire to experiment with whatever he or she finds. This can be toys, paints, crayons, or perplexing-looking items such as sockets and flexes. Your first priority should be to ensure that the room is as safe and as enjoyable for your child as possible, your second to provide adequate storage space for toys and all the other paraphernalia that small children invariably accumulate.

Young children love bright colours and will often show preference towards reds, yellows and oranges (not surprisingly—this is the end of the colour spectrum that babies and small children see best). If the size, shape and aspect of the room will take it, you might like to incorporate one or more of these colours in your scheme, either on the walls or on soft furnishings and furniture. If you want to tone down these colours, choose corals and pinks instead of red; peach or apricot instead of orange; and primrose or cream for yellow. For a really vibrant effect, accent your chosen colour scheme with its complementary in the colour wheel (in other words, red and green, orange and blue, and yellow and purple), but make sure that you choose a complementary that is the same tonal value (i.e. intensity of colour) as your main colour or you may find your scheme looks too discordant. Such décors, although great fun, can be difficult to pull off, and you may prefer to stick to a harmonious scheme, where two or three colours, or more, are used, which lie next to each other in the colour wheel.

The decorative technique introduced in this chapter is painting on furniture. This does, of course, include stencilling, but here the emphasis is on transferred images (using tracing paper), which are then painted in freehand (the special project in this chapter shows you how to do this). Pick favourite characters from fairy tales or storybooks and transform even the humblest piece of furniture into something special and unique.

DECORATING IDEAS

A toddler's room should be stimulating and fun, and the walls, for example, can be much more vibrant than those of a baby's room. You could have fun painting each wall a different primary or try spattering in two or three contrasting colours for a really lively effect, an easy technique which is easy to master (see page 145). If you don't want to cover all four walls with spattering, you could try it on only one, or even just on the floor. For example, paint the floorboards in a dark base colour then spatter with bright, strong colours on top. For a less vibrant wall finish, spatter in more subdued pastel colours or complementary tones, such as mid- and light blues, or sponge (see page 142) the walls in, say, dusky pink and white for a softer effect.

If you would prefer to leave the walls white, then you could add interest with colourful posters, cut-outs, and anything else your child enjoys. Large cut-outs can be made out of light wood or thick cardboard, then fixed to the walls or suspended from the ceiling. These could be letters of the alphabet, clouds and rainbows, or butterflies and flowers. Paint them in appropriate colours which go with your general scheme for an effect that is lively and can be changed easily at a later stage.

Page 34: the Beatrix Potter characters featured on the curtains and cushions in this delightful room provided the starting point for decorating the furniture and wall. The characters were traced and then scaled to suit the different-sized pieces (see pages 149–50), before being transferred and painted. Care was taken to match the colours throughout to create a totally coordinated look.

Right: in place of a freehand mural, use stencils to achieve much the same effect. Here, pools of spotlight were painted in first to provide well-defined areas for the stencilled clowns.

Constantly changing decoration

A good idea might be to paint the walls down to a real or imaginary dado rail with your chosen finish or colour. Then, below the rail (if you don't already have one, mark it simply as a line, or stick a length of wood moulding to the wall) paint the wall with white vinyl emulsion, and allow your toddler to use this section as a canvas. Your child will have hours of fun making patterns on this part of the wall, and it certainly saves ruining expensive wallpaper. Another idea might be to paint this section of the wall with blackboard paint. Felt-tip pens or crayons will wipe off either surface without too much difficulty.

If you don't want the walls scribbled on at all, a temporary solution is to attach large sheets of lining paper to the area below the dado rail and then replace them as they are filled up. Or stick on cut-outs (which you can then varnish over), perhaps all depicting the same theme (such as a farmyard or a jungle scene). You can use the same technique on walls, ceilings and smaller items, such as cupboard doors.

Murals of character

Toddlers love colourful pictures, and you might like to paint a bold mural on an otherwise plain white wall, or across some fitted cupboards. Or think on smaller scale: one or two characters painted boldly in a corner will often suffice, and can more easily be painted over later on when your child's tastes change.

Another idea is to paint a changeable mural. Cover the walls and ceiling with sky and a border of grass at the bottom of the wall. Then pin or stick cut-outs of cars, animals or trains on to the grass, and birds, kites or aeroplanes on to the sky area.

As far as subjects for murals are concerned, your child will probably have some favourite characters from nursery rhymes or storybooks which you could use as a

Above: blue skies and undulating hills and fields are the ideal background for a changeable mural. On walls painted with eggshell white, a can of blue, cellulose car spray paint was used to create the patches of blue sky; the green is diluted green poster paint rubbed on with a crumpled newspaper. Cut-outs made out of white card were also painted with poster paints and stuck in place with re-usable adhesive.

Left: door and wall are skilfully integrated here by continuing the nursery-rhyme theme over both. The painting on the door is especially eye-catching, and throughout there is a lively sense of movement and fun.

starting point, or take a general theme, such as a circus or woodland folk, and paint details around the room. Again, an easy background for such murals is simply to paint sky and grass on the wall (or walls) and then people it as you like. You could then echo the theme by painting characters on, say, the roller blind or curtains, which, when pulled down or drawn, also form part of the mural. There are other areas of the house, too, that you might consider for such treatment; a bathroom, for example, is an ideal place for lively, colourful schemes – making bathtime more fun.

Following a theme

If you have painted an ambitious mural across one wall it is bound to dominate the room, so do not be tempted to add boldly patterned duvet covers, blinds or curtains and floor coverings. But you could try recreating one of the same characters in a repeating pattern on plain curtain and duvet cover fabrics. Trace the characters on to the fabric and then colour in your design, using fabric paints or fabric crayons (see page 134). Finally, if necessary, place a clean cloth on top of the painted fabric and iron it to fix the pattern.

Above and right: sponged yellow walls provide the background for another playful variation on clowns in this colourful children's bathroom. The ready-made paper border of clown motifs at the top of the wall are echoed by the hand-painted clowns adorning the tiles surrounding the bath and wash basin. Non-toxic enamel paints (see page 133) are ideal for painting ceramic surfaces, and come in a wide range of strong, durable colours.

You can create all sorts of patterns in this way, of course, and your child may well want to help colour the characters. If this is the case, you could draw the outline of the characters and your toddler could help colour them in. Do this on paper, using transfer fabric paints, inks and crayons, so that you do not waste fabric when discarding poorly executed designs. When you are happy with your motifs or patterns, simply iron them on to the fabric in a pleasing arrangement.

Regular patterning

If you do not wish to include a mural in the room, but you still want to introduce some lively shapes and patterns, your first choice is to look at the wide range of wallpapers and paper borders specially designed for children's rooms. For a more individual scheme, try mixing two or three different designs together, but make sure they share similar colours and tones or the finished result may be too lively!

Another idea, if you want to create your own pattern in the room, is to stencil (see pages 138–41) motifs such as farmyard animals along the dado line or at the top of the wall, or stencil birds flying high above on the ceiling. Expand on this theme by using the same stencils to make a decorative feature elsewhere on the wall, as well as on blinds or curtains, and perhaps also on the duvet cover or a decorative border on the top sheet using fabric paints.

Alternatively, stencil bold shapes down the curtains and all over the floor to make abstract patterns. A geometric pattern stencilled across or around the edges of the floor can look particularly effective, especially if you are stencilling on bare sanded or bleached floorboards, or make an attractive border around a plain-coloured or canvas rug (using heavy-duty canvas, doubled and stitched for strength).

Above: selected from a range of wallpapers and paper borders specially designed for children's rooms, this room has made imaginative use of them to create a totally individual look.

Left: the restrained decoration in this pretty bedroom contrasts strongly in style and content from the bedroom above. A simple stencilled border of boy and girl holding hands encircles the room, linked by a curving line of delicate hearts, and a picture of the two continues the theme further down the wall.

Right: a child's bed has been transformed by the imaginative treatment of the window blind directly behind it. Pooh and his balloon have also been used to embellish the headboard, while the shelving features Pooh and his friends.

Drawing the furniture together

When you are painting your child's room, don't forget that decorating the furniture too may really add the finishing touches. If the pieces are in good condition, you will not need to repaint them. However, if they are in need of retouching, try painting all the pieces the same colour: eggshell white is ideal if you intend to add more decoration, otherwise you could try a sponged or spattered effect (see pages 142 and 145) (only use the latter if you have not already spattered the walls).

You could also think about giving the bed an imaginative treatment. There are any number of special 'theme' beds available on the market, but these tend to be expensive, so why not have a go at transforming the bed yourself. This could be something as simple as painting a favourite character on the wall behind the headboard, to transforming a four-poster into a covered wagon by attaching a canvas canopy and two 'wheels'. A bunk bed could be changed into a ship's cabin with port holes painted on the wall behind it, or a fort, or an old-fashioned bus.

Lighting choices

Bright light is preferable in a toddler's room as he or she may want to play in the room and will need to be able to see clearly. Introduce a central, overhead light and cover it with a colourful and exciting lampshade: try stencilling a jungle scene around the edge, or some aeroplanes flying around it. If your child is afraid of the dark, fit the central light with a dimmer switch so that you can leave it on all night. Alternatively, place a lamp on the bedside table. Safety nursery lights are available, which give a dim glow for night time and which can be turned up for a brighter light if necessary. You can also buy light-sensitive automatic lights, which switch on when it gets dark and off when it gets light. Glow lights plug straight into the socket and give off a gentle, reassuring light at bedtime.

MURALS

Woodland creatures, such as hedgehogs, squirrels and rabbits, often appeal to this age group, and work equally well in small and large murals. You need not paint these creatures in an absolutely realistic setting—try placing them in a semi-circle of leaves and flowers (this will also help to contain your composition) or in and around a simple tree shape.

Another idea would be to try a jungle scene in the style of Rousseau's paintings. Amid a mass of dense foliage, paint the faces of animals peeping out (these can be traced from books and scaled up—see page 150). Wrap snakes around the branches of trees, and paint monkeys swinging from branch to branch. Include parrots among the foliage, and, if you feel you can carry it off, have an explorer peering ahead through binoculars.

Or try painting scenes from under the sea (the background can easily be painted in using a large decorator's brush to form some bold, undulating bands of sea green)

Above: vigorously painted in bold colours and with a sure hand, this wonderful fantasy scene is made more lifelike by the swinging shutters and painted windowsill.

Left: this playroom was changed into an undersea grotto by the bold use of fabrics and paint. The ruched emerald-green material strung across the ceiling creates a wonderful water canopy for this ambitious mural, and provides the ideal setting for the underwater play house.

complete with exotic underwater plants and various creatures of the deep, buried treasure, and even the odd merman.

Alternatively, try painting a huge doll's house without the façade so that you can see into every room. Incorporate your child's room in the doll's house, complete with his or her own furniture and toys.

Whatever style of mural you decide on, paint the characters or motifs in the scene so that they fit in with the shape of the room. If, for instance, the room contains an arch, paint a tall character in keeping with the theme of the mural—a giraffe, for example—so that it leans against the arch. Likewise, if the walls have exposed wooden beams, make the most of them by painting a row of characters along one or two of them with their legs dangling over the fronts, as though they were sitting on the branch of a tree.

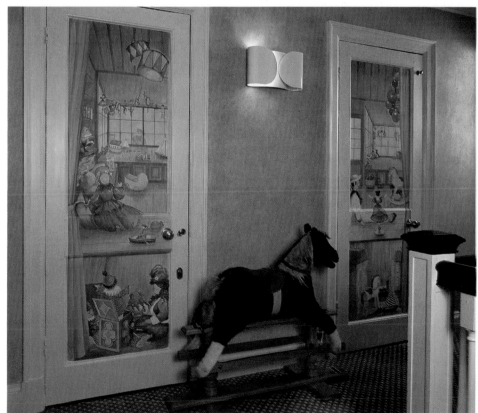

Opposite page: the mural that covers all the walls in this fantastic bedroom creates a fairy-tale world for its lucky occupant. To give the room an Alpine cottage atmosphere, imitation wood strips were painted on every wall. The triumph of the room, however, is the trompe-l'oeil green walkway peopled with well-known childhood characters.

Above: this tiny painted mural on the fireplace takes the theme of horses evident elsewhere in the room.

Left: these two doors have been transformed into illusory panelled rooms full of dolls and other toys. The subdued colours are in sympathy with the carpets and ragged wall.

PAINTED FURNITURE IDEAS

Toddlers take a lively interest in the world around them; they love bright colours and rooms with a lot going on in them. So try painting the furniture in the room too. If your toddler has a toy box, start with this. Paint his or her name on the lid, or, if you are feeling more ambitious, cover it with motifs that your toddler likes or with images of the toys inside.

If your toddler is sharing the room with another child, all the furniture could be decorated in such a way as to enable each child to identify the pieces or parts of pieces that 'belong' to him or her. Let each

child choose a different colour, motif or character and then decorate the pieces appropriately, such as chairs, chest of drawers and so on. Alternatively, you could paint the name of each child on the pieces.

Although your aim will be to decorate the furniture in a playful, stimulating way, remember to consider the overall effect. The pieces should not fight each other for attention, nor should they clash. Rather, they should look as though they belong to each other, while at the same time retaining their individuality and complementing the rest of the décor.

Right: this toychest was stencilled (see pages 138–41) with motifs popular in Victorian and Edwardian times: rocking horses, and stars and crescent-shaped moons. To finish, the chest was coated with polyurethane varnish tinted with a rust-coloured paint to give it an antique look.

Complementing the walls

Perhaps you have already painted an extensive mural along one wall with a scene inspired by the countryside, complete with squirrels, rabbits, badgers and foxes. If so, it will not be a good idea, for example, to paint all the furniture bright red and add bright yellow aeroplane motifs. Instead, paint the furniture white and decorate it with characters taken from the mural. You could have rabbits running all the way around a small circular table; the headboard of the bed could feature a group of badgers; a series of foxes could be running across a chest of drawers or around a small freestanding mirror; each small chair could have a different character painted on its back; or you could paint characters on each of the long doors of a wardrobe. To apply your designs, use the transfer method shown in the next section (see pages 48–53).

In contrast, perhaps your walls feature borders and a large frieze along the bottom section containing abstract shapes, interspersed with numbers and letters—all painted in bold primaries. Now is your chance to paint the furniture a primary colour to link the pieces to each other and to the walls. Then stencil or transfer print all sorts of similar shapes and textures on selected surfaces. Try to make some kind of pattern over the larger expanses, such as the bedhead, and to line with a contrasting colour wherever possible to tie the pieces together. Otherwise, you may find the overall effect is too much of a jumble to be pleasing to the eye.

Linking the pieces

It is always a good idea to give all the pieces of furniture in the room the same base colour, painted in the same style. If you want your characters or motifs to stand out dramatically, then simply paint the furniture eggshell white. If you do not want

the characters to stand out quite so much, then paint the furniture in a colour that blends or contrasts with the walls, or try a distinctive paint finish, such as dragging (see page 143).

Alternatively, make the background colour appropriate to the motifs themselves. For example, try painting the pieces sky-blue to provide a suitable background for motifs of various sorts of aircraft, old and new, plus the occasional cloud, sun and rainbow. Or paint the pieces yellow-green, and cover them with exotic animal motifs, such as lions and tigers, jaguars, monkeys and parrots.

Placing the motifs

Try to involve your toddler when you are choosing colours and motifs, so that the room reflects his or her interests and likes.

Above: a child's swing mirror complete with little drawer was first given a top coat of white eggshell paint. The basic outlines for the balloons and friendly teddy bears were then traced in position and painted using non-toxic enamel paints (see page 133).

If your child loves teddy bears, work up some drawings featuring them in different poses, perhaps incorporating a different element in each, so that you can vary the motif over the pieces of furniture without ever straying from your theme.

Do not be tempted to paint the motifs at random. Instead space them at equal intervals to make a simple overall pattern on each of the pieces. For example, the chest of drawers might feature two clowns at either end of the top drawer, one clown in the centre of the middle drawer, and two clowns at either end of the bottom drawer. Alternatively, they might march in a diagonal line down the chest over the drawers.

With a long, thin motif, such as a steam train with many carriages, you would need only one motif per drawer. Start the train from opposite directions as you proceed drawer by drawer down the chest, so that on the first drawer the train puffs from left to right, on the second, it trundles from right to left, and on the third from left to right again. Make sure that each image starts from the edge of the drawer. Such a motif would also make a good edging for a toddler's round table simply by extending the number of carriages so that the train runs all the way around. Practise drawing the train along a curved line on a piece of card until you have mastered the problem

Above: the delicate shape of this small wall clock demanded a suitably sympathetic approach. Dragged (see page 143) in pastel pink and embellished with pastel-coloured motifs, the paint treatment is entirely in harmony with the object.

Right: this beautifully painted chest of drawers bears looking at closely, not least for such charming details as the butterflies with 'keyhole' bodies and the petal formations surrounding each chest knob. The charming scene on each drawer is skilfully framed by edging the chest in grey-blue, and the linear motif repeated either side of each drawer subtly draw the eye to the centre.

of perspective (see pages 154–5). Then trace the train on to the table in segments.

Of course, you do not need a long motif to make a border, whether circular or square. All you need do is repeat one image at regular intervals around the table. A running animal—cat, dog, mouse, rabbit—works well in this context, as it lends movement. A simple geometric pattern will look equally effective if primary colours and abstract shapes make up the decorative theme throughout the room.

Painting small scenes

The bedhead is an ideal place to paint your toddler's favourite character (or characters). Try making a scene in the centre that is particularly appropriate to bedtime, such as the Sleeping Beauty or the princess and the pea, or simply a fairy asleep in her bower. A hammock with Brer Rabbit lying full stretch on it, or a cat in a basket, an owl with one eye open, are also popular choices. Experiment with the scene on paper first and then trace your final version on to the bedhead. Paint it one colour at a time, to build up the picture gradually.

Once the image is dry, consider framing it. Try using a leafy or flowery border, or stars. Follow the curve of the bedhead carefully and, if you use individual motifs for the border, make sure that they are regularly spaced.

The images on the bottom end of the bed and down the legs should tie in with the one on the bedhead. Perhaps this time the cat is awake, or the owl has his other eye open. To finish, paint very small images of the character along the bottom and down the legs of the bed.

The element of surprise

Toddlers love visual surprises and you might like to build in a few of them when you are painting the furniture. For example, you could hide tiny images of mice

Above and left: by trailing a banner from each of these rabbit-piloted biplanes, each child's name could naturally be incorporated into the design. Further decorative details include back-end views of similar machines on the headboards, and primary colours painted on the turned legs of the bunk bed.

in the larger scenes, so that your child can try to find them. Or you could paint on both sides of the wardrobe doors. Perhaps Little Bo Peep could be searching vainly for her sheep on one side of the door, while on the other side of the other door, there they are, just waiting to be found.

PROJECT TWO
A NURSERY CHAIR

This nursery has a very friendly, welcoming atmosphere. The practical, hard-wearing sandy-brown carpet could easily be the floor of a warren; the cream-coloured walls add to the rustic feel of the room – already suggested by the beams and the mural painted in faded browns and greens on the wall – without making it dark; while all the furniture, including the fireplace surround, is painted white to make the most of the light that enters the room from the single window above the chest of drawers.

The furniture has been painted with a white eggshell base to give a cohesive look that also minimises any feeling of clutter in such a small room. The specially painted Beatrix Potter curtain material was then used as a starting point to paint similar characters in gentle pastel colours on all the pieces.

If you want to make an exact copy of a character from a book or magazine, it is worth pointing out here that you should always check first whether or not the design is in copyright with its publishers. Most publishers are happy to give permission free of charge so long as your design is not for commercial use.

All the furniture to be painted was prepared to give a smooth surface (see page 137) and coated with an oil-based primer. After leaving it for 24 hours to dry, the pieces were then painted with a base coat of white eggshell, which provides a smooth, impermeable surface for painting with enamel paints (as shown in photograph 1 on page 50). You may feel that the furniture that you are decorating requires more than one coat, in which case, allow

1. The chair was first painted with a white eggshell base coat to provide a good surface on which to display the various decorative motifs.

eight hours for the first coat to dry before adding the second. Then leave for at least another 12 hours before decorating with the motifs, using non-toxic, lead-free Humbrol enamel paints (see page 133).

Enamel paints diluted with standard regulation white spirit were mixed with white on an old plate used as a palette to make them softer and sweeter. Pastel blue and pink were chosen for the decorative rules and scrolls, which were painted on each piece of furniture to 'hold' the design and link all the disparate pieces subtly.

The chair was painted first: pink was brushed on to the tops of the legs and in narrow bands around the centres to em-phasize their neat, turned nature. Across the middle bar on the back of the chair and across the top bar on the reverse side, a scrolling motif was positioned and traced in the centre and painted in pink. The chair was then personalized by tracing the owner's name across the top bar (as shown in photograph 2).

To do this yourself, first draw a straight line on a long piece of 60g tracing paper. Trace the letters one by one with a sharp pencil from an alphabet book. Make sure that the bottom of each letter is sitting on the ruled line and that the letters are an equal distance apart from one another. Cut out the word and mark the point on the piece at which you want to position it. Draw on a horizontal guideline and place the tracing paper so that the base of the letters sits on the line. Now check that the word is correctly positioned before fixing it in place at either end with low-tack masking tape. Slip a piece of supercharged, waxless carbon paper (which does not smudge and is available from artists' suppliers) behind the tracing paper and go over the letters carefully with a very hard pencil. When you have finished, remove the tracing and carbon papers to reveal clear outline letters ready to be painted.

The same method was used to transfer the character motifs to the other pieces of furniture. Several characters were traced, enlarged using the scaling up method described on page 150, and then each figure held up against the furniture to establish the best combinations for each piece. For the chair, six characters in six poses were chosen: one on the front of each leg and two on the reverse of the tall legs. The motifs were lined up carefully, each pair positioned on the same horizontal line (as shown in photograph 3 on page 52). To do this, hold the tracing and carbon papers very steady so as not to smudge the motifs. If you do make a mistake, however, wipe off the pencil mark with a damp cloth. Once you have transferred all the characters to the piece, remove any dirt and smudges using a damp cloth and a little liquid scourer. This will also help to provide a sound surface, or key, on which to paint.

2. The letters were very carefully positioned on the back of the chair, to make sure that they were central – both horizontally and vertically.

The letters and motifs were then painted one colour at a time (as shown in photograph 4). Enough of each colour was mixed to finish the decorations on the chair as it is very difficult to match exactly a colour that you have mixed. Using a fine paintbrush, paint carefully within the line. Apply one colour at a time and work from left to right if you are right-handed, and from right to left if you are left-handed. This should ensure that you do not smudge the paint with your hand as you continue painting. Leave each colour to dry for two hours before applying the next colour. Continue until all the 'flat' areas of colour are filled in. Leave to dry thoroughly, then add the details: the eyes, nose, buttons, etc. Finally, with a very fine brush, paint a dark outline around the figures so that they are well-defined. Leave to dry. Then, if you see that you have made a mistake, wipe it with a damp cloth dipped in white spirit and paint the motif again. Never try to tamper with a motif before it is dry. When the paint is dry, you will have a perfectly durable surface that can stand plenty of scuffs and knocks. Don't be tempted to varnish any furniture painted in this way as it will quickly yellow the colours underneath. If a bit of paint does come away, simply touch it up with the enamel paints.

The rest of the white-painted furniture in the room was painted using exactly the same techniques and character motifs as

3. Each of the character motifs was traced onto the chair using 60g tracing paper, supercharged, waxless carbon paper, and a sharp hard pencil.

4. Each of the characters was made to stand out clearly in relief by painting their outlines in a dark brown.

for the chair. For the chest of drawers, a symmetrical design was carefully created, using six Beatrix Potter figures.

Finally, a border of small figures was painted on the toddler-sized table top (as shown in photograph 5). To frame the design, and link the table to the other pieces in this child's room as well as to the pelmet and curtain ties, a simple border of pink and blue lines was painted close to the edge all around the table top, and tiny, delicate blue motifs depicted on the tops of the legs. Delicate scrolling, echoing that used more boldly on the chair, was used to link the figures of the border to one another and to lend movement to an otherwise static design.

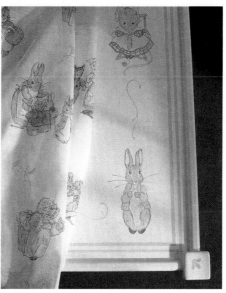

5. The table-top design took its inspiration from the curtain material in terms of colour, character motifs and border.

TODDLERS: Basic Room

In this toddler's room, the baby's cot has now been replaced with a sturdy bunk bed, complete with guard rails around the top bunk (but do remember that it is not safe for a child of less than six years' old to sleep on the top level). Later on, this can either accommodate a younger brother or sister, or a friend who wants to stay overnight. The nursing chair and trolley, having served their purpose, have now been removed and replaced with a brightly coloured cabinet with large plastic trays for storing all sorts of smaller playthings. Later on, this cabinet can be used to form part of a work station for studying and homework. The shelves, which were originally used to store equipment for changing the baby, now provide a home for larger play items. The special, child-proof covers are still in place on all the electrical sockets, and the window bars continue to be an important safety feature.

BASIC REQUIREMENTS

Toddlers have an insatiable curiosity and many are quite fearless; they are also highly mobile. So safety is the major consideration when you are designing a toddler's room or redesigning a baby's room to cope with the needs of a toddler. Toddlers may not, in fact, spend that much time in their bedrooms, but it is vital to make them as secure and practical as possible.

Reassessing the floor

As toddlers spend a lot of their time on the floor, it is as well to consider this area first. If you are starting afresh, consider vinyl-coated cork tiles or cushioned vinyl, which are both hard-wearing, reasonably attractive and easy to clean. Polyurethaned wood, which may appeal to your taste, is another option (it can be painted and stencilled beforehand), but do make sure it is absolutely smooth and splinter-free, and even

then it may be too slippery underfoot for your toddler. Rubber stud flooring is another possibility as it is soft, noise-resistant and comes in a range of colours.

Carpets are warmer and softer, of course, but show wear and tear more easily. If you do choose carpeting, make sure that it has a smooth finish; long or shag pile is too impractical for playing on with toys. Carpet tiles might be the answer here, as you can replace worn or badly stained tiles singly. All the same, if you decide on these, go for mottled effects that conceal stains, or choose one of the new carpets on the market that actually 'repel' stains, making cleaning them very easy. Or consider a mixture of soft and hard floorings to differentiate between the various areas in the room. For example, you could have carpeting in the sleeping area and a wipeable surface in the play area.

Left: this bold, bright room also contains many practical features. The red and yellow flooring is made up of hard-wearing vinyl tiles, and the bed is in fact a pair of stacking beds, with the second bed's mattress used as a backrest. Storage space is provided by the pine store chest under the window, and the curtained-off table in the far corner is used to hide a host of toys.

Above: this delightful wagon bed in this toddler's room also provides more storage space beneath it. The large, built-in cupboard beyond has been carefully designed to accommodate clothing as well as many different kinds of toys and games.

Adding furniture

The furniture is likely to grow with your child, both in size and amount. A toddler will transfer to a bed from a cot at some stage, depending on size and how adept he or she is at climbing out. At first you may find a bed guard (a movable bed side which slides under the mattress) useful to stop your child falling out of bed. (Some cots have removable sides, while others convert into small beds which can last the child up to the age of six or so.) You may find that a bed will not fit in the same position in the room as the cot, calling for a complete rearrangement of the room. If space is limited, consider buying a bed with drawers underneath, or bunk beds, which come in a variety of shapes and sizes and can accommodate friends to stay or a younger brother or sister as the years pass. Ensure, however, that there are guard rails on bunk beds – and don't allow a child of less than six years old to sleep on the upper level. Also ensure that the ladder has smooth slats and can be fixed firmly or permanently in place. Whatever type of bed you choose, ensure that your child has a firm, good-quality mattress, to encourage the growth of a straight spine.

If you have only a small chest of drawers and a small wardrobe to begin with, you will now need to add furniture that provides extra storage space or replace the pieces with larger ones. Make sure that any fresh furniture you acquire is perfectly solid and cannot be pulled over. You will also want to add some shelves for books, ornaments and toys. If the room is large, you might like to add a small table and chairs to form a play area, and your toddler will undoubtedly need a toybox. However, at this age you may find that your toddler wants to play wherever you are in the house, and that the bedroom is reserved for sleeping.

With more items of furniture in the room, there is a danger that the room will look cluttered. To create a more cohesive look, give all the pieces the same painted treatment. If, however, you want to create two distinct areas in the room, for example the sleeping area and the playing area, you could paint the furniture in two different styles or colours.

Common sense dictates that furniture should be as wipeable as possible, as spillages and breakages are inevitable. Decorate furniture with non-toxic, lead-free paint (see page 133) as toddlers like chewing everything in sight – even chairs. Also ensure that any upholstered furniture in the room is fireproof and conforms to regulation standards.

Working lights

If you have not already done so, consider introducing task lights into the room for a play or work surface and a light for looking at books. If you have already installed track lighting then train the spotlights in the appropriate directions. A simple alternative to try is clip-on spotlighting. It is best not to have freestanding lamps in a toddler's room, as they are easy to knock over. The best solution for bedside reading is to fit wall lights by the cot or bed.

Toddlers can be afraid of the dark, so make sure that the lights have dimmer switches, so that one could be left on all night if necessary, or install a low wattage night light. It is also a good idea to make sure that there is one light switch within reach of your child in case he or she wakes up frightened in the middle of the night and wants to put the main light on.

Storage ideas

As your child grows older, storage space becomes much more of an issue. Clothes will still fit in an average chest of drawers and a wardrobe, but toys will probably be accumulating by this age. Weed out outgrown toys and put them away or give them away. A large toybox or even a large plastic dustbin or wastepaper basket (you can buy them in bright, attractive colours) will help solve the problem for the larger items. But encourage your child to be tidy by putting particular toys in particular places; for example, large toys in a toybox, crayons and paints in a shoe box.

If there is enough space in the room, you could try building a simple storage system at a low level out of, say, tea chests. Sand them down and paint them in different bright colours, then set them on their sides, one next to the other and one on top of the other to make two rows (but make sure these are securely attached so that there is no danger of the top row toppling over). On a smaller scale, you could make a system of wire baskets, laundry baskets or office trays, ideal for storing small and medium-sized toys and games, painting and drawing materials, and even items of clothing.

Safety first

If you have not already done so, it is probably a good idea at this stage to install vertical window bars (these discourage climbing), but make sure that they can be removed quickly by an adult in an emergency, such as fire. Other safety options for the windows are grids, removable bannister rails, which look attractive too, or childproof locks. Bars should not be more than 8 in (20 cm) apart.

At this age, it is more important than ever to install socket covers on electrical sockets, or, even better, to place electrical sockets up high out of reach of tiny hands. Make sure, too, that flexes are fixed very firmly to the walls, just above the skirting board, so that curious fingers cannot pull them away. And ensure that there are no trailing wires or flexes.

It is also advisable to fit safety gates at the top of the stairs to ensure that your child does not slip and tumble down them.

Below: the problem of storage was solved in this room by the inclusion of brightly coloured laundry-type baskets fitted into a specially designed storage rack. Each basket has a stencilled piece of paper stuck to it reflecting the contents, thus helping the child to put away toys easily and correctly.

EARLY SCHOOL-AGE 4–9

By school-age, your child will probably have much firmer ideas about how the room should look and will more than likely be interested in any decorative schemes you are planning for the room. Now is the time to really involve your child, who may in any case need little persuasion in suggesting a favourite colour or characters to decorate furniture, walls and even fabrics. At the same time, you will have to think about such practical things as a decent table and chair for work and play, proper lighting, and you may also want to reassess the storage situation as your child's belongings grow with his or her interests (these are all discussed at the end of this chapter—see pages 78–81).

The main decorating technique covered in this chapter is painting on fabric. There are many ways to do this, using fabric pens, special fabric paints and brushes, as well as techniques such as sponging, spattering and transfer-printing. Transfer-printing is particularly useful as it allows you to experiment with your design on paper before committing yourself to fabric, and the design can be filled in carefully before transferring it. One of the main merits of fabric-painting is that it enables you to produce designs that are in keeping with the rest of the décor in terms of content and colours. Unusual and distinctive children's pillowcases and sheets or duvet covers, for example, can be difficult to come by and are often pricey—by painting these yourself, you can be sure of producing something that is individual and which coordinates exactly with the rest of the room.

DECORATING IDEAS

Page 58: a charming, 'period' theme room has cleverly combined antique and modern pieces in a harmonious whole.

Below: the theme for this room is clearly nautical. The ship motif on the curtains and bedspread was used as the basic design for decorating the headboard, bedside table and chest of drawers.

Opposite page: designed for two lively children, the décor in this spacious room has deliberately been kept minimal and bright. Useful storage features are the two large drawers underneath each bed for individual toys and games.

School-age children will not only have a huge fund of ideas for decorating their rooms, but they will probably want to help decorate too. Work with your child to create a room that he or she will feel is truly personal as well as practical. Erect shelves in every nook and cranny, and ensure that there is enough storage space for toys at a low level so that your child becomes used to putting things away. Establish a different identity for each type of toy by painting, for example, each drawer of a chest of drawers a different colour or painting a simple picture of what each should contain on the front: a doll might feature on one drawer front; a train on another; and building bricks on a third.

Choosing a theme

Theme rooms are always popular with children, and they also provide you with a useful starting point when trying to devise a completely fresh scheme. Depending on your child's interests, such a room might be based around a nautical theme, natural history, horses and horse-riding, music and dance or simply concentrate on popular cartoon characters or figures from favourite storybooks. The degree to which you carry the theme throughout the room depends on the amount of time and energy you wish to spend on it. In a nautically inspired room, for example, ship motifs might be limited to fabrics, such as curtains and bed linen, and painted on selected items of furniture, or you could extend it to include a border of stencilled motifs on the wall at dado or picture-rail level.

On a larger scale, a mural of a schooner sailing on the high seas, complete with leaping dolphins and spouting whales, will definitely set the scene; or if your child is a keen bird watcher, you could cover the walls with examples of different and exotic species of birds.

Creating visual fantasies

Your child may have a favourite play pastime. If he or she has a 'Wendy' house or 'home corner', you could fit it in with the overall design of the room by painting a complementary mural behind it. If you have a large expanse of wall, which in any case requires some special treatment to make it more hospitable, try painting a street of houses, with more houses behind, retreating gradually up the hill. Place the Wendy house at one end and watch it merge with the others in the street, so that at first glance it appears in line with the others. To make such a mural effective, you will have to be adept at creating a three-dimensional look, or *trompe l'oeil* (see pages 154–5), which is more difficult to master, but possible with perseverance.

Right: the Winnie-the-Pooh bedspread was the starting point for smaller decorative features in this room, such as the motif on the headboard and tiny characters around the frame of the pinboard.

Below: again, the fabric design provided the decorative theme for this pretty bedroom. All the furniture was sponged a delicate pink first and then the bow motif painted in using non-toxic enamel paints (see page 133).

You could transform this into a place of total make-believe. Perhaps your child is fascinated by *The Adventures of Alice in Wonderland*. If you have plenty of white wall at your disposal, trace scenes from the book and then transfer these to the walls using the scaling-up method (see page 150). On one side you might have the Mad Hatter's tea party; on another the White Queen and the chess pieces; in one corner the Cheshire Cat might be found grinning; and in another the White Rabbit could be running. The individual characters could also be painted on to various pieces of furniture to extend the theme.

Visual jokes

At this age, children love visual jokes. So, on a smaller scale, painting mouseholes in the skirting board, spiders hanging from long webs in the corner of the room or on a blind, a mouse running along the bottom of one wall, or a bat hanging upside down from a *trompe-l'oeil* beam will probably all be well received.

If you have fitted a roller blind rather than curtains you could paint on a 'hide and seek' visual surprise. For example, you could paint a railway track on the wall on either side of the window, with a steam train puffing along the piece of track on the left, and a small country station on the right. Then, on the blind, using fabric paints (see page 134), you could continue the track, but paint it running across a bridge which crosses a steep, rocky ravine. In the day time, when the blind was rolled up, there would be no hint of the landscape described in the centre image, but at night the full story would be there for all to see.

Involving your child

Whatever you decide to paint, make sure your child is involved in the planning stages, so that you incorporate favourite characters, and so that he or she feels really involved in the creation of the room. A sure-fire way of making the room feel personal is to paint the letters of the child's name on the door, and on some of the pieces of furniture.

If you do not feel up to painting a mural or *trompe l'oeil*, there are still many painting techniques that will enliven the room, some of which your child can become involved in too. Stencilling on to walls and

fabrics is simple and can be very effective. Either use a ready-made stencil, or let your child choose a character or motif, such as a favourite cartoon character, a teddy bear, bird or flower, and trace this on to stencil material (see pages 138–41).

Block printing is a technique all school-age children will be familiar with and eager to try out on the walls, and perhaps even on the floor. They will be used to cutting

Below: another nautical theme room, this time created using stencils. Stencilled dancing sailors and waves form a lively border on the wall, and the jolly hornpipe jigger on the duvet was stencilled on using fabric paints (see page 134) and then given an appliquéd shirt as a finishing touch.

Above: the headboard on this charming four-poster is, in fact, *trompe l'oeil*. The mice tripping along the top and peeping through the heart-shaped hole not only add a sense of fun, but also encourage the eye to believe in this artistic 'deceit'. Other delightful details include a mural of squirrels used to turn the top beam into a branch.

Above right: the headboard and chest of drawers shown here were dragged (see page 143) and then painted with floral motifs taken from the bedspread.

shapes out of potatoes and using cross sections of apples to dip into paint and then print on paper. Let your child try cutting shapes out of sponge to make repeating patterns along the wall at shoulder height. You could help your child create a crude but effective water mural in this way. Paint a background of blue-green sea with stylized waves, then in the foreground print fish and other sea creatures, such as crabs and starfish, cut out of sponge. Alternatively, simple abstract sponge shapes, dipped in different colours, might make an interesting base to the walls of the room.

Painting the furniture is another way to introduce individual character into a room. If your child hankers for a soft, pretty look, try dragging (see page 143) or colourwashing (see page 147) one or more pieces in a pastel colour and then add a simple motif

such as flowers or bows, perhaps taken from a design elsewhere in the room, such as the curtains or bedspread.

Considering the whole design

Your child might well be determined to have a certain wallpaper, featuring a favourite comic hero, or one that is covered in aeroplanes or trains. If so, use the main character or motif as your starting point for decorating the rest of the room. Trace the character or characters in all their different guises, scaling them up or down using a grid (see page 150) or photocopier with an enlarging and reducing facility, then transfer them to, for example, the chest of drawers and sides of the desk. Paint the characters one colour at a time, using non-toxic enamel paints (see page 133).

You could have one or two characters or motifs featured in many different sizes, seen from many different angles all over the room. You could paint trains puffing across the curtains and around the duvet and in a mural along one wall to echo a circuit set out on the floor. You could paint the bed to resemble the train engine, with the bedstead the funnel, and you could have many little trains puffing hither and thither on the desk, chairs and chest of drawers.

MURALS

Although murals are usually painted on walls, there is nothing to say that you cannot create a mural on a floor or ceiling if you wish. At the opposite end of the scale, a mural can be quite small, particularly if you limit it to a distinct area, such as window shutters or a blind.

Small-scale murals

An old, disused fireplace might be an ideal site for a small-scale mural, or cupboard or wardrobe doors, even an alcove. Or simply frame your mural on the wall, like a picture or as a window. A toybox or chest could be painted with a scene containing the characters housed inside, or, more unusually, a table top painted as if set out for a tea party (as shown on page 154).

Floor murals

To paint a convincing mural on the floor, you should choose a scene that is appropriate for ground level. For example, you could transform the floor into the deck of a ship, complete with coiled ropes and hatches. Extend the mural a few feet up the

Left: an ordinary, disused fireplace has been transformed into an exotic temple. A door has been attached to the grate and beyond it is revealed a tiny display of toy figures set against a night sky. Above it, the highly decorative arabesque draws attention to the entrance, while linking up with the line of bright yellow arabesques along the mantelpiece. Lions guard the entrance at either side and stylized green leaves march up the columns.

Opposite page: this ambitious and detailed mural has transformed a bedroom into an old-fashioned railway station. Even the ceiling has been painted with sky and birds.

Left: horse-racing scenes painted on the sides and top of this large toy chest are beautifully set off by the strong black background.

Below: a small-scale mural of a cricket board and players clearly reflects one of the interests of the child who uses this bedroom.

walls to show the sides of a galleon, battleship or yacht, with the sea splashing over the sides and the wheel at the front. Alternatively, you could paint the floorboards the colour of the sea and introduce unusual fish and other sea creatures swimming in its translucent waters.

Or try painting a snakes and ladders board that your child could actually play a real game on. In the same way, a racing track or railway track painted on the floor all the way around the room would also provide the impetus for indoor play.

Ceiling murals

You should choose subjects for the ceiling with care, and, preferably, in character. You could paint a blue sky with cotton wool clouds, below which could hang your child's aeroplane models. Likewise the cosmos with galaxies and objects spinning through space would be ideal for showing off your child's hand-made spaceships and satellites, which you could suspend below.

FABRIC PAINTING IDEAS

Many of the paint effects you would normally think of using on walls can be used on fabrics too. The duvet cover or bedspread, the pillows and cushions, lampshades, the curtains and perhaps a plain-coloured or canvas rug can all be decorated, using fabric paints, inks and crayons (see page 134). Before you launch into your design, however, consider the styles and colours used on the other surfaces in the room and paint the fabrics in a manner and shades that complement them.

Adding texture

If you have already sponged the walls in delicate blues and greens, you could continue this scheme on the duvet cover and curtains so that any decorative motifs painted on top of any of these surfaces will stand out strongly in relief. On a white or pale-coloured material, repeat the technique using a natural marine sponge and a suitable fabric paint for the material you are painting (see page 134). Fix the design by ironing the material face up, after covering it with a scrap of spare material.

Alternatively, so that the fabrics make more impact, sponge them in contrasting reds and oranges or in darker shades of the same blues and greens. Or try sponging pillowcases and cushions in bright, contrasting shades, and larger expanses of fabric, such as curtains or blinds, in more subdued combinations.

You can create another subtle, textured effect by spraying closely related colours over the fabric. Dilute the fabric paint if you are using a diffuser (a very much cheaper version of the airbrush), so that it does not clog up with paint. Alternatively, if you are using a toothbrush or nailbrush to spray a fine layer of paint over the surface (see page 145), load it moderately with paint. If you want to define these sprayed areas, use low-tack masking tape to mark off a specific shape. Spray paint of one colour over the exposed surface area to begin making, say, a pattern of blocks of colour. Overlap the blocks until you are satisfied with your built-up design. Taking this idea a step further, buy or cut your own stencils of a particular motif and spray-paint over these to create a more formal or intricate pattern. Whatever method and pattern you choose, be careful not to spray-paint over any other surfaces.

Simple patterning

If you want the duvet or curtains to make more impact in the room, try spattering them with bright colours for a Jackson Pollock effect. The strong but random forms of the paint are always eye-catching, but best used on larger rather than smaller areas of fabric for greatest effect. The technique is easy to master, and your child will probably enjoy helping you. Once again, make sure the other surfaces are covered before starting.

Below: the simple stencilled design around this lampshade creates a focal point for this part of the room. Framed top and bottom by a dark blue border, which was painted in with the help of masking tape, the Scottie dog stands out well among the long grass and pretty flowers.

Another technique that your child will be more than qualified to help you with is block printing. He or she will probably be adept at printing from cut vegetables (especially potatoes) dipped in watercolours and printed on to paper. Your child could try printing small pieces of fabric first of all on, for example, cushion covers, and build up to bigger items as he or she becomes more adept.

You can also use all sorts of found objects, such as keys, soles of shoes, coins, matting—anything with a textured surface or unusual shape. If you wish, you could make your own raised shapes out of thick card to print on to the fabrics in the room.

Plan out the pattern you want to make before you start. If you are printing material to be made into curtains, it is probably more pleasing if the pattern runs in columns from the top to the bottom of the material, although by all means experiment with different effects. Try printing a series of squares, one set within another and glued to a block of wood, down the length of the curtain, alternating the colour as you proceed. Or try making a pattern using different-shaped keys. On the duvet cover or bedspread, try printing a series of footprints, using your child's shoes.

Rather than buying expensive curtain material, you may prefer to buy lengths of sheeting (in cotton, or polyester and cotton mixed), which comes in a good range of plain colours.

Repeating motifs

If you have chosen a theme of painted motifs for the furniture or in borders on the wall, you might prefer to paint the same motifs on the fabrics in the room as well. These might be stencilled numbers or letters, which can look particularly effective if they are set within thin rules or bordered

Above: this handy bag for carrying a host of small toys uses the same motif as that on the lampshade opposite, but here the design was hand-painted using a stippling technique to introduce a textured effect. As a finishing touch, tiny fabric bows were sewn on each Scottie.

with a rule of flat colour on either side. For a more artistic look, try stencilling numbers and letters falling randomly down the curtains to end in a jumbled heap at the bottom.

For a much more formal look, stencil a border of flowers, birds or animals around the edges of a plain-coloured or canvas rug or on the bed cover and pillows, that links with a stencilled border on the wall. Use contrasting colours so that they stand out. This is particularly effective if you want to give the room a rustic look, and complement it with stripped wood furniture and walls painted in pastel shades.

Or you could make an equally spaced pattern of aeroplanes or brightly coloured hot-air balloons floating all over the bedspread. Paint one on the lampshade of the

bedside lamp, too, or on a central paper lampshade, to finish the picture. To complete the effect, you can make hot-air balloon lampshades (or buy them) and hang a little basket below for a small soft toy.

Transfer printing

A simpler idea, if you are not yet very confident and do not want to experiment on long lengths of material while trying different designs, is to use the technique of transfer-printing, although this is only suitable for man-made fabrics. Again, your child could help. Simply try out patterns on pieces of paper first, using transfer-fabric crayons or inks (see page 134) for the outlines and transfer-fabric paints to fill in the shapes. Then, when you are happy with the colours and style of the design, place

Right: a spider blind for children who delight in the offbeat. The straight lines of the web were pencilled in first using a ruler, and the curves drawn in with a compass. Use either fabric pens or paints (see page 134) to paint in the lines (if necessary, place masking tape either side of the pencilled lines to ensure that they are absolutely straight when painting in).

Above and left: the American football duvet cover design was stencilled in blue and red, and complements the dynamic footballer painted on the wall adjacent. A star motif was stencilled at the centre of the circle of footballers, and stars and stripes were stencilled around the edge of the cover to make a fitting border that also links the design with the stencilled flag on the pillowcase.

the paper pattern face-down on the material you wish to decorate, and press it with an iron for about a minute. Take care not to touch the fabric directly with the iron, which you should set to medium.

To use the same pattern again on another section of the material or another surface, simply colour in the paper pattern again—otherwise the colours will be too pale—and press on the surface as before. Repeat until the whole surface is covered, then look at the whole thing carefully. If there are some spacey areas, fill them with smaller patterns executed on paper and transferred in exactly the same way.

Theme ideas

If you are confident of your drawing skills you might like to try copying characters from your child's favourite books or television programmes on to the duvet cover, using fabric crayons and fabric paints. Try painting small groups or individual characters engaged in characteristic activity. If your child is interested in sport, try transferring an American football player on to the duvet cover. You could even repeat the figure for a really dramatic effect.

Another interesting idea for the bed cover—but one that requires some artistic ability—is to make the whole of the surface look like a honeycomb. Paint bees all over it once the basic pattern is dry, and continue the theme by painting bees elsewhere in the room—on the furniture and in a mural. Or try painting a prehistoric landscape containing a range of animals and brightly coloured plant life.

PROJECT THREE
PAINTED BED LINEN

Cars provide the main theme in this lively, stimulating bedroom. A repeating pattern of red, blue and green cars, all pointing in different directions, covers the walls. One of the duvet covers and the pillowcases also feature this motif, using the same colours. On the other duvet cover, a much more ambitious road and countryside scene was created, using fabric paints and several different objects to block print. The following pages show how a matching pillowcase design was painted. If you have not painted fabric before, a pillowcase might be a good place to start, as the design area is small and the fabric will be easy to stretch out tautly to work on. When painting bed linen, remember to slip a piece of card in between the layers to prevent the paint seeping through. If you do not want to attempt a duvet cover all in one go, lay the fabric out over a large table, and move it along section by section to paint.

For full colour and durability, most fabric paints should only be painted on natural fibres, such as cotton, linen and silk (always check the manufacturer's instructions), and must be fixed after painting with a medium-hot iron (but again, check the manufacturer's instructions). The only exceptions to this rule are transfer paints and pens (see page 134), which come out full strength on man-made fibres, but are considerably weaker on mixed fibres, such as polyester cotton.

Fabric paints come in an enormous range of colours. However, you need only buy a few to achieve a wide variety of colours, as you can make up many in-between shades by mixing colours. Here a

1. A selection of the fabric paints, brushes, sponges and other 'found' objects that were used to paint both the duvet cover and the pillowcase. Always wash the saucer before placing the next colour in it, or the two will become confused. Also, if you are mixing colours, be sure to mix up enough of each one to cover all the places in which it appears in the design.

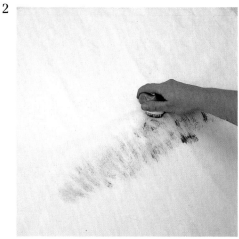

2. Achieve a rough grass texture with bright green fabric paint and a scrubbing brush.

3. Cut out a square piece of sponge-backed card for the basic house shape.

4. Once the paint is dry, add the roofs and chimneys, and windows and doors with triangular and small square pieces of card.

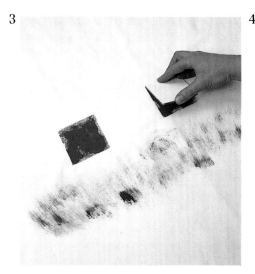

5. Paint the trunk of the tree with an ordinary, quite thick, paintbrush and dark brown fabric paint. Sponge on the foliage, using the abrasive side of the sponge for a highly textural effect.

6. Using a small round piece of wood, make small, decorative flower heads in red with a blue centre.

7. The pillowcase and duvet designs make perfect partners.

basic palette of black, white, red, blue, yellow, green and brown was used to paint the duvet cover and pillowcase (as shown in photograph 1); a wide range of shades and tones can be made from these. Pastel colours are easily obtained by adding colour to white (never try it the other way around as you will probably find that you require an enormous amount of white paint to lighten the tone sufficiently).

Taking the duvet cover scene as her starting point, the artist worked up a simple house and grass design for a matching pillowcase, making sure that the scale and colours were accurate. The three main colours of the room – red, blue and green – were chosen, together with dark brown. To print the shapes and textures required by

the design, the artist used a scrubbing brush, some sponge-backed card, round and square pieces of wood, and a sponge. Before using them, however, she first tried out the colours and the effects created by the different printing objects on an old piece of cotton cloth. This is always to be recommended before embarking on the fabric proper.

To keep the fabric taut, the pillowcase was stretched out and secured to a flat surface using low-tack masking tape. The surrounding area was protected with cloth in case of spattering. The grass was the first part of the design to be tackled. The green paint was poured into a saucer and a scrubbing brush dipped into it. Any excess paint was wiped off on to the piece of protective cloth. Then, pressing hard, and dragging the brush in short vertical movements, a foreground of grass was created (as shown in photograph 2 on page 74).

Two simplistic houses to match the houses on the duvet cover were started next, well above the still wet green paint. Taking a piece of sponge-backed card, the artists dipped it in a saucer of red paint, removed the excess on the spare piece of cloth as before, and pressed it down firmly twice (as shown in photograph 3 on page 74) to make two red squares.

Once the red paint was dry, the artist took a triangular piece of card and dipped it in a saucer of blue paint to form simplistic roofs on top of the houses. Little square pieces of card were used for the chimneys, doors and windows (as shown in photograph 4 on page 74).

A stylized tree was painted between the two houses, using an ordinary brush for the trunk, and a piece of an abrasive kitchen sponge cut into a circle for the foliage (as shown in photograph 5 on page 74). The sponge was dabbed several times at the top of the tree trunk, overlapping the edges to create different densities of colour.

Finally, little flowers were depicted in the spaces between the houses and the grass, using the end of a round piece of wood (you could use a dowel rod) and red and blue paint for the petals and centres (as shown in photograph 6 on page 74).

When the paint was completely dry, the fabric was covered with a piece of cloth and pressed with the iron set to medium-hot, to fix the design (according to manufacturer's instructions). When doing this, it is best to protect the ironing board with old, clean sheeting. The finished pillowcase design reflects the duvet cover design perfectly in colour, shape and texture (as shown in photograph 7 on page 75).

For the duvet cover, the artist first sketched out on paper the road, rail and

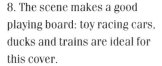

8. The scene makes a good playing board: toy racing cars, ducks and trains are ideal for this cover.

9. Although the Beetle car design on this pillowcase does not match the duvet cover, it reflects the wall design and is of the same theme as the cover.

countryside scene. When she was satisfied with the design, she copied it on to the fabric, using a soft-lead pencil. Various pieces of card, bits of wood, a scrubbing brush, a cut sponge and a matchbox end were used to paint in the design, one colour at a time.

The railway track was painted first, using a fine brush for the lines and the end of a matchbox for the tracks. The solid parts of the design – the winding grey road, and the pastel blue pond – were filled in using an ordinary paint brush. The matchbox end was also used to paint the white lines in the middle of the road. The grass was created with a scrubbing brush, the square house with pieces of card, and the flowers with a round piece of wood (as shown in photograph 8).

Another of the artist's designs can be seen on the car pillowcases (as shown in photograph 9). Inspired by the 3-D Volkswagen Beetle hanging above the bed, she painted three similar Beetles on the cover using the same colours as those used in the car design on the wallpaper. By painting the wheels and windows black, the cars were made more solid looking, and therefore stand out well against the white background of the pillowcase.

EARLY SCHOOL-AGE: Basic Room

The most important room change at early school-age is the introduction of a well-lit work surface for various activities and interests. Although homework won't play a large part in your child's life at this stage, later on it will become more important and it is just as well to choose a proper desk at this point that will see your child through to the teens. Here, a large desk with a cupboard either side, providing plenty of storage space, has been installed in front of the window to make good use of daylight with a proper reading lamp for evening. The filing cabinet used in the toddlers' section for storing toys and games has now been turned into a place for filing away such things as drawing and painting equipment, albums, and so on. A pinboard to the left of the desk provides space for pinning up favourite pictures and postcards, and a solid, foldaway chair combines comfortable seating with practicality.

BASIC REQUIREMENTS

Your child starting to go to school should provide you with the impetus to re-evaluate the room. You can now remove the safety bars at the window and reassess storage systems in view of the undoubted increase in toys, games, painting and writing equipment, books and clothes that your child will have. A proper desk could also make an appearance.

Increasing the storage

If you are moving your child to a different room in the house, or if you have just moved house, you might consider changing the furniture. At this age, your child will require a full-size wardrobe and chest of drawers. If two school-age children are sharing the same room, consider installing some fitted cupboards, which are usually the most efficient use of space.

Buy a bed, bunk beds or separate beds with drawers underneath, so that this space—which would otherwise be wasted—also serves as a storage area for bulky items such as bedlinen and blankets.

Fitting in the bed

If the room has a high ceiling, consider a climbing frame-like structure for the bed with several landing stations on different levels so that going to bed is fun (the very bottom level can be used for much needed storage space). Make sure safety rails on the stairs and platforms are included, and ensure that there are no sharp or rough edges. Paint the tubular frame a bright colour so that it becomes the main feature of the room. Make believe that the frame and bed is a castle and that the rest of the room is a moat: paint the floorboards blue-green to simulate water.

If your children share a room, save space by installing one or two bunk beds. If the room has an alcove, fit the beds into

Left: to maximize the playing and working areas in this large room, a bunk bed was introduced and set against the wall in one corner. The whole of the area beneath the three windows is taken up with a work surface, and a fitted cupboard was installed in the play area to store toys and board games.

storing toys and games. If there is plenty of space and you have not already done so, now might be a good time to build an open-plan storage system on the lower part of one wall so that your child has no trouble using it.

Keeping everything tidy

You might like to install a storage system of boxes or wire racks at child level to encourage your child to keep possessions tidy. Use an alcove to advantage by installing a shelving system for toys and books. Use brightly coloured baskets—different colours for different kinds of item—or paint shelves different colours, and encourage your child to stand books upright by making interesting bookends. If you are a budding carpenter, cut animal shapes from wood and paint them in cheerful colours.

Or try erecting shelves, varying the heights of the spaces between them, and then fitting vertical wooden dividers between the horizontal shelves to create boxes or segments. Paint the whole system a bright, cheerful colour and help your child to create a sensible system of storage.

Above: taking advantage of the alcove created by the chimney breast, a freestanding shelving unit has been installed within easy reach of the desk. Bright red plastic baskets on the shelves and on the floor provide easy storage for smaller toys and games.

that to create maximum floor and play space; if not, place them against one wall. Alternatively, if you have a large room, you could set the bunk beds in the centre of the room to create two areas—one for play and one for resting and sleeping. If you are going to incorporate bunk beds into the design of the room, it is often as well to make them a major feature of the room, as they will tend to dominate anyway because of their size.

Storing books and toys

For books, you will need to erect shelves or acquire a freestanding bookshelf. If you choose to put up some shelves, make sure they are low enough for your child to reach the books—and put them back.

Toys are still best kept in a toybox of some kind, unless space is very tight, in which case you will have to designate a place in the wardrobe or under the bed for

Right: here, another coordinated room has built-in shelves to accommodate lots of books, and a large, built-in cupboard for clothes and larger toys.

For example you could put large toys and games at the bottom, with, say, board games in one 'box' and train set in another, then put toy cars or dolls in another segment higher up, and books in another at a similar level. Mark each segment in a different colour and then draw up a list to put on the pinboard saying which articles correspond with which coloured segment.

Alternatively, make a storage system using industrial shelving for a practical, hard-wearing and hi-tech look. Or you might consider buying brightly painted filing cabinets to store some of the larger articles. By installing two low-level cabinets side by side with a space between and placing a formica top over the two, you have a ready-made desk, complete with storage space.

Incorporating a work surface

A room for a child of this age should include an area to work in and a work surface. The space does not have to have a separate identity from the rest of the room: it is probably best if the area does not seem too formal, but is integrated with the play area. So do not install an officious-looking desk and chair; rather buy a simple table, perhaps painted a bright colour, and matching chair—make sure both are low enough—which your child will like and to which he or she will feel drawn.

Ideally, place the desk in an alcove or between bookshelves so that your child feels enclosed—cosy and secure. Fix a blackboard or pinboard above the desk, or provide an easel. Boards on wheels are another idea both as a pinboard and a movable room divider.

If you cannot fit a freestanding desk or table comfortably in the room, consider buying a work and sleeping station, in which the bed is considerably raised above ground level and the desk is fitted into the space beneath (much like a bunk bed, but with the lower bunk removed). Make sure that you fit a safety rail to such a bed so that there is no chance that the child will fall out when asleep. Alternatively, buy a bed with a table that extends from beneath the mattress, which your child can pull out whenever he or she wishes to use it. Another idea is a table that folds down into half its normal size, which might provide the answer if space is severely limited.

Improving the lighting

Whatever work surface you choose to include in your child's room, make sure that you also provide good lighting for your child while seated at it. Place an adjustable reading lamp on the desk, or train a spotlight from a track on the wall. If the room is short of task lights, try fitting clip-on spotlights to the book shelves or storage system. You could also incorporate freestanding lamps in other parts of the room now that breakages are less likely. Place one on the bedside table—which might also hold toys, books and decorative items, such as a child's clock.

Below: shelving and a small bureau and seat have been cleverly integrated into this awkwardly shaped room. The step up to this area subtly and neatly separates it from the rest of the room, and it is cosily enclosed by the slanting ceiling.

PRE-TEENS 9–12

The range of decorating ideas in the first section of this chapter reflects only some of the many and varied schemes that might suit children in this age group. However much *you* would like a particular look, some children will be perfectly happy simply to cover every wall surface with posters and pictures (in which case it is probably best to leave the room well alone!). Others might like a bright, modern look which can easily be achieved using strong, clean colours and some of the paint effects suggested in the following pages. Others still might hanker for a pretty, country-style room – the main theme of this chapter.

You needn't live in the country to achieve this look: a combination of the right colours, soft furnishings and decorative treatments will quickly suggest a country theme, even if you live in a terraced or semi-detached house in the middle of the city. The various country styles (for example, rustic and country house) are in any case interpreted fairly loosely here; what all the rooms suggested and illustrated have in common is their country 'feel'. Not everyone can afford completely to refurbish their child's room with pine furniture, or hang expensive chintz curtains in the country-house manner; but, as this chapter shows, with a little imagination and some special decorating techniques up your sleeve, most rooms can be transformed into a rural retreat. If your furniture isn't suitable for stripping, embellish it with stencilled fruits and flowers; colourwash or rag the walls for a suitably faded, soft look, then use the same stencils to make an attractive border at picture rail height. If the floor is carpeted, add one or two inexpensive rugs in a suitable design to give interest to this area. Otherwise you could leave the floorboards sanded and varnished or you could even paint them and create a distinctive edging of stencilled motifs before varnishing.

DECORATING IDEAS

At this age children's tastes are as diverse as their interests. Many will consider themselves nearly grown up and will therefore want to cast off bright primaries and childish murals. Instead they might want a sophisticated paint finish for both walls and furniture, or they may hanker after a mellow, cottagey look. Others will want their rooms to be fun and to reflect their sporting or leisure interests. Others still will prefer an ultra-modern, hi-tech look.

Modern looks

If your child prefers a modern look, then primary colours and geometric shapes will be appropriate. Offset multi-coloured, abstract wallpaper with plain-coloured sag bags and furniture. And try painting the furniture in one or two bold primary colours—say yellow and red—for a really bright and breezy look. If you have not already done so and it is time for a new floor surface, fit wall-to-wall, short-pile mottled carpeting for a warm, practical look, and add rugs for splashes of colour.

Another idea is to leave the walls plain white or a pastel shade and try spattering or stippling the furniture (see pages 145 and 146). A desk spattered in greys and black will look both fun and hi-tech. Make sure that the desk lamp complements this look—matt black would be best—and add some novelty desk items for the final touches. A large, coloured peg or clip for

Page 82: the bedside table, toy chest, desk, bookshelf and window seat in this sophisticated, country-style bedroom were all stippled (see page 146) in pale pastel blue and then decorated with discreet floral motifs.

Right: more country cottage than country house, this four-poster features simple stencilled (see pages 138–41) ribbons and bows. The same design appears on the chest of drawers and in the wall border.

Opposite page: this bright, modern room uses navy and white striped fabrics to make a strong impact against white walls and ceiling. Cleverly space efficient, the bottom bunk doubles as a racing-car track at playtime.

Above: the colourful superhero cut-outs on the walls of this dynamic bathroom add a flexible touch of frivolity to a functional room. The practical, pillar-box red stud flooring, bath, pipes and roller blind are guaranteed to wake up the most bleary-eyed child first thing in the morning, while colour-coded mugs, towels and toys make bathroom quarrels a thing of the past.

holding paper, and a pen holder with your child's name painted on it would all go well with such a desk. Extend the fun element to the wall in the work area by painting a large, brightly coloured pencil balancing on its point. Then, running along the bottom of the wall, just above the skirting board, paint a larger-than-life ruler.

Erecting a bold structure in the middle of the room to raise the bed to a mezzanine level can work well in a modern-looking room. This can be bought in kit form and erected easily or you can have one built out of wood. Then paint it the same primary colour as the rest of the furniture. The structure could also serve as a work area if you built a desk into it at floor level. This would be a great space saver and would make a strong focal point for the room.

If the room has a high ceiling, you could hang a canopy of brightly coloured material from one side of the room to the other. This would help reduce the height of the room, provide something in the way of sound proofing, but most of all offer another point of interest, especially if it is lit from above with a central overhead light. Measure the length and width of the ceiling and add 3 in (8 cm) to each side. Cut the material to the larger size and pierce a hole in each corner. Oversew the raw edges of the holes, so that the material will not fray. Fix 1 in (2.5 cm) hooks into each corner of the room at the tops of the walls, then place the holes in the material over the hooks. Make sure that the material does not hang too close to the overhead light, otherwise it will get scorched or burnt.

Peopling the room

Your child will probably have favourite characters—both real and fictional—that he or she would love to be surrounded by, and which you might like to draw and paint across one wall. Alternatively, you could paint the favoured superhero in the centre of the duvet cover: catch him or her in a dramatic pose, for example, face-on, hurtling towards the observer, with one arm outstretched and fist clenched. You could even try your hand at a graphic 'zap' or 'pow' to add a dramatic touch.

If you feel ambitious, decorate the walls, furniture and fabrics with a whole host of heroes and heroines. They could assume different poses according to their position in the room.

Perhaps your child prefers less auspicious cartoon characters and there is a whole world of popular cartoon characters to offer you suitable inspiration. Just flick through some of your child's favourite comics or magazines. You could trace figures on to the chest of drawers getting up to various antics, or they could be portrayed in a range of poses along the bookshelves, on the desk, and on the curtains and bed cover. If your child is really fond of a particular cartoon character, why not try recreating a whole cartoon strip to make a border along the wall.

Creating new worlds

Children of this age may well want the décor in their rooms to reflect their current main interests. For example, your child may be fascinated by spacemen and rockets. To reflect this, you could, for example, paint a rocket in its launching pad on, say, either door of the wardrobe, with spacement walking in and out. Then, along one wall you could paint a mural of a moon scene with the spacemen and the landing vehicle moving across the moonscape. If you do not feel up to tackling such a mural,

why not try drawing the stars, planets, the earth and galaxies as seen from the moon. Your child could actually use it like a board to enact space games using counters for rockets: stick them to the wall with a re-usable adhesive.

If you don't want to paint a mural at all, try simply decorating the walls and ceiling with a selection of stencilled stars placed at random (for added effect, you could paint them in gold and silver). The result will certainly be eye-catching.

Another idea is to paint a large-scale

Above: this fantasy bedroom has a night-sky ceiling painted the same deep blue as the carpet and liberally stencilled (see pages 138–41) with stars. The theme is carried throughout the room, right down to the cushion star and moon on the four-poster bed.

map of your local area on the wall, featuring sites well-known to your child, such as the school, your home, shops, the houses of friends and so on.

Or your child may adore submarines. If this is the case, you could decorate the room as though it were the inside of a submarine, with grey-painted walls, stencilled number, bulkhead lights and a 3-D periscope fixed to the bedhead. Or you could make the whole room into a castle, with crenellated walls, slits for arrows, and arms and armour painted on the walls.

Simple patterns and shapes

Combining a number of patterns and colours in the same scheme is another way of creating a striking and distinctive effect, but unless you have a very sure eye for such things, limit yourself to a total of two or three different patterns in the room, preferably with a linking colour running throughout. Ready-made patterned wall-

papers and fabrics provie a huge range for you to experiment with, or make your own patterns using simple shapes made out of pieces of wood, fruit and vegetables, as suggested in the previous chapter (see pages 72-7): an activity your child will enjoy too. You can make up trees and flowers, birds and butterflies, houses and walls, ships and trains out of simple shapes, using colour upon colour, shape upon shape to form separate, colourfully patterned areas, such as friezes on walls, on curtains and on furniture.

Stencilling is another way of making eye-catching patterns very simply. Perhaps your child is interested in a sport. A border of black and white check footballs would be easy to make using stencils, or motifs of tennis rackets, hockey sticks, rugby balls or table-tennis bats. Use them individually on furniture, repeat them to make a border on walls, or use them to make patterns on the bed cover or curtains.

Opposite page: the various patterned papers and fabrics used in this lively, colourful room have been confidently mixed together, while red provides the linking colour throughout.

Left: on a gentler note, a basic scheme of pastel-colour butterflies on a pale blue background is enlivened by the introduction of subtle variations.

MURALS

By this age, your child will have quite a sophisticated visual sense, so a mural in his or her room will not only have to reflect latest interests and fads, but may also have to contain a wealth of accurate detail and be skilfully drawn and painted —not a project to embark on unless you are confident of your artistic skills!

Characters from comics and cartoons are always a good source to draw on, and they are often particularly popular with this age group. They are also, fortunately, relatively easy to increase in scale, since most comic-strip and cartoon characters are very simply delineated, mainly consisting of clearly defined areas of flat colour. If your child has a number of favourites, why not put them all together in one fantastic scene, or, on a smaller scale, concentrate on a single, dramatic figure placed in a suitably eye-catching spot?

If your child is into all things American, why not paint an American scene or montage? Paint a hamburger joint in the shape of a bun and hamburger, and fill the street with bright lights and neon street signs. Include a soda bar, a brightly coloured juke box, Chevys, and pick-ups, and people wearing baseball sweatshirts.

Your child might prefer another world altogether. You could try your hand at creating a space-scape peopled with aliens, together with weird and wonderful plant life, or try recreating a fairground scene. Paint a traditional roundabout centrally on one wall, showing the various brightly coloured horses, cockerels, dragons and mythical beasts being ridden by children. Then, on either side, you could paint a series of other attractions such as coconut shies, dodgems, a haunted house, and in the distance the big wheel.

Right: any budding ballet dancer would love these graceful figures on their wall, and their linear quality makes them particularly easy to scale up and paint in. Use stencils to introduce tiny decorative motifs, as shown here.

Far right: dividing the wall into two planes neatly limited the size of this mural area to the lower part of the wall. The humorous cartoon character was then painted in using a basic palette of black, yellow, red and white.

COUNTRY-STYLE IDEAS

By the time your child reaches nine or ten, he or she may well favour a more natural-looking room, perhaps to make a complete change from the bold primaries and abstract patterns so loved just a few years earlier. There are several country styles that you can use—from the truly rustic look taken from the colours of nature (shades of green, brown and yellow, with subtle textures and simple patterns), to more sophisticated, formalized schemes, where furniture is painted in pastel colours and embellished with delicately coloured flower motifs. Further afield, there are the Scandinavian country styles, and particularly that of the painter Carl Larsson. Here,

floors are bare or painted to match the walls, walls are painted in washed-out colours, and all the furniture is painted too – choose from blue and white, green and red, even warm yellow and rust. For a really authentic look, the bed should be built in and have shutters (complete with a little heart-shaped motif cut out of each shutter).

The country mood

For the walls you might try hanging wallpaper that features a small-print design of, say, birds or flowers. This will be ideal if the room is large but rather overpowering if it is small. In this case, restrict cottage

Below: the walls of this cottage bedroom were sponged (see page 142) in pale apricot over an ivory base. As the floorboards were in good condition, they were simply sanded down and varnished and two matching cotton-weave rugs laid down.

prints to the curtains or soft furnishings and instead paint the walls. Try colour-washing (see page 147) in light pastel shades of yellow, apricot or peach. Apply a white ground to the surface, then, when it is dry, cover with a coat of oil- or water-based paint (but remember not to use a water-based paint over an oil-based ground) that has been thinned with white spirit or water, as appropriate, in the colour you prefer. The effect will be to give the room just a hint of translucent colour.

Alternatively, sponge the walls (see page 142) in creams and yellows or greens and yellows, or try ragging or rag-rolling (see page 148) in pale pastels for a slightly more sophisticated look.

Naturalistic borders

To complete the rustic look on the walls, try stencilling a simple border or frieze using naturalistic motifs (or buy a ready-made border). You can buy ready-cut stencils of flowers, trees and animals or you could design a rustic-style motif on paper and cut your own stencil from it (see pages 138–41). Keep the design straightforward so that there is a natural simplicity about the overall look of the border, and use subdued, dusky tones to recreate the charms of that slightly faded country look.

As an alternative to stencilling, try block printing a border on the wall. Glue a simple naturalistic motif, such as a small leaf, berries or a flower, made out of thick card on to a block of wood. Then paint the raised shape in a darker shade of one of the base colours used on the wall, and stamp it firmly on the wall. Repeat over and over again, renewing the paint as required until the border is complete. You could make several woodblocks of varying design but using the same theme for all and alternating the shapes along the border: paint each raised shape in a new shade to accentuate the difference in design.

Decorating the floor

The floor of, for example, a traditional country cottage would more than likely feature a canvas rug or Indian dhurrie placed on sanded and varnished floorboards. Alternatively, stain the boards to complement the colourwashed, sponged or ragged walls. You may wish to stencil a border on the floor that relates to the border on the walls. Intertwining flowers and leaves are suitable for a traditional cottage border, or you could try a repeating pattern of, say, acorns. Make sure that you

Above: inspired by Carl Larsson's work, this charming attic room already possessed all the necessary ingredients for such treatment – tongue and groove ceiling and walls and a slanted niche for the bed. Washed all over with eau de nil, the room was then stencilled using variations on two basic motifs.

Above: the jewellery box, swing mirror with small drawer beneath and hairbrush were all dragged (see page 143) in delicate pale pink over a white eggshell base, and then decorated in pastel shades with flowers echoing those found in the dressing table and curtain fabrics.

Right: oak panelling sets the scene for this romantic country room. The dusky pink colours chosen for the drapes over the four-poster bed, the dressing table, curtains and comfy armchair are entirely in keeping with the overall mood of the room.

space the motifs at equal intervals and make sure they are square to the wall.

You could also apply a stencilled design to a plain-coloured or canvas rug, if it does not already have one. Create a naturalistic centrepiece, such as a huge basket of flowers or fruit, and frame it with a naturalistic border. If you do not have a canvas rug, why not paint the central area of the floor in a base colour and then stencil a design on top to give the impression that there is a rug in the centre of the room?

Motifs and patterns

To complement the walls and floor of the country-style room, hang curtains in a matching pastel shade but featuring a pretty cottage print. The duvet cover or bedspread could be made of the same print, or you could stencil your own design on to all three elements. Choose a naturalistic

motif again, but use it small in a regular pattern over the fabrics. An owl, a hedgehog or a squirrel stencilled over and over again would look appropriate, and you could stencil a border of leaves on the duvet cover and pillow cases.

Alternatively, you could try your hand at a freehand painted design on the soft furnishings, using fabric paints and crayons. Try painting interweaving flowers of sinuous lines in the style of William Morris. Otherwise, paint related flowers in a regular pattern, perhaps with their names included underneath.

Country-style furniture

You will not want to put modern-looking furniture in this room. Instead, choose stripped pine or oak pieces; this is the place too for a four-poster bed, complete with draped curtains. Leave the pieces as

they are or sand them down well and coat with polyurethene varnish for a more hard-wearing finish. Plain wood is appropriate if you feel that there is already enough pattern and texture in the room. Otherwise, sand the pieces and decorate them too with naturalistic motifs such as flowers, bouquets, individual birds and animals. Treat all the pieces in the same way to create a cohesive look, often essential when one room contains many separate and completely different items of furniture.

If you cannot afford good pieces of pine or oak furniture, or if the wood is of poor quality, it is probably best to paint them to conceal any faults or imperfections. In this case, paint all the pieces of furniture in the room in the same manner so that they look cohesive. Paint them a dusky or deep colour that complements the other colours in the room, and try using a more stylized technique, such as dragging or combing (see pages 143 and 144), to give them weight. You can then either leave them plain or stencil (see pages 138–41) or paint freehand motifs on top.

It is difficult to make modern fitted cupboards look 'rustic', particularly as these are not usually an authentic feature of country cottages. Either treat them as though they were part of the wall and paint them in the same colour and style, or defy convention and make a feature of them. Try combing the panels (see page 144) and lining them, while sponging the surrounding wood. Then, if you like, add a rustic motif in the centre of the panels.

For the more sophisticated country-house style, paint the furniture white or pale pastel (this could be dragged, see page 143), then highlight with floral motifs copied from old design books or make up your own. Alternatively, if you have already chosen a pretty floral fabric for the curtains, you might like to copy this as your design feature on the furniture.

Above: a detail of the same room shown below left reveals a charming grandfather clock. Painted in a ground coat of pale pink eggshell, its decoration was partly inspired by the large garlands of pink ribbon featured on the curtain.

Left: the modern bureau featured here was softly stippled (see page 146) in palest blue to give it a more rustic look and then painted with floral and ribbon motifs to tie it in with the rest of the décor.

PROJECT FOUR
A COUNTRY ROOM

The essence of this country-style room is floral. The deep blue-green ragged walls, with stencilled classical eighteenth-century garlanding, provides a rich, textured background for the bold floral patterning of the curtains and upholstered chair, and the white-painted furniture embellished with floral motifs, to create a sophisticated 'country' room. The curtains and upholstered chair feature a rich, large-patterned floral design in blue-green and pink on a warm, creamy background. The luxuriant, pleated curtain fabric speaks of comfort and warmth, while the floral patterning on the white-painted furniture is more restrained and sparse, yet clearly owes its inspiration to the floral design on the fabrics. The whole effect is pretty yet dignified, and the room would undoubtedly last well into the teenage years.

The walls were decorated with a technique known as 'ragging off' (see page 148). They were first painted with a base coat of cream-coloured eggshell. Then, once dry, an oil-based glaze (see page 133) tinted a dusky blue-green was applied in broad strips with a standard decorators' brush. Using a scrunched-up soft rag, the artist dabbed firmly and evenly on the still-wet glaze to remove some of it (as shown in photograph 1 on page 98). She continued across the wall (taking in the light switch), working in bands from top to bottom and swapping the rag for a new one as soon as it was loaded with paint, creating a random yet formal patterning with the cloth. Always dispose of used rags in an airtight container, but not a polythene bag, as these are highly combustible.)

1. An oil-based glaze, tinted a blue-green, was applied thinly over one section of the wall, and then ragged off with a scrunched-up cotton cloth.

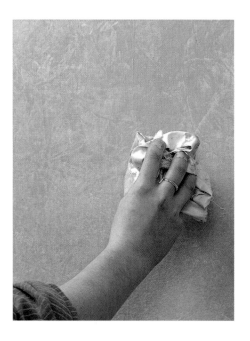

When the ragged finish was dry, a classical eighteenth-century garland design was stencilled in each of the corners of the wall (as shown in photograph 2). The bows and ribbons were stencilled in two shades of blue; the paler shade was painted in first and while still wet the darker shade was added with a separate brush to create areas of shadow. The result is a lively sense of movement over the whole which also lends depth and an almost three-dimensional reality to the design. Emulating the colours used in the patterning on the curtains and chair fabric, the artist then stencilled in the leaves and flowers.

The pieces of furniture were each primed and given a base coat of white eggshell. Taking her inspiration from the patterning

2. A sophisticated garland design was worked up on paper, cut out to make a stencil and then transferred to the corners of the walls painted in blues, green and pink – the colours of the room.

3. The white-eggshell-painted chair and dressing table were embellished with the same floral motifs, which took their inspiration from the curtain.

on the curtain, the artist worked up small floral motifs on paper first. These outlines were then traced on to each of the pieces, starting with the chair, using tracing paper over supercharged waxless carbon paper (see pages 52–3) and transferred by rubbing over them with a hard pencil. The motifs on the chair back were carefully positioned to make a symmetrical pattern. The ribbon motif in the centre at the top of the chair back links the two halves of the pattern, continuing the movement, and echoes the ribbons on the cushion seat and the wall. In pride of place, in the centre of the chair back, a full-blown rose was transferred. After transferring the designs, the motifs were painted one colour at a time (see pages 52–3), using the green,

blue and pink shades that appear throughout the room. Their outlines were not defined in a dark colour as in the toddler's chair (see page 53), in order to create a more delicate effect (as shown in photograph 3). (There are masses of floral motifs you could copy or trace and use in your designs. Choose one or two different sorts of flower-head and restrict yourself to three or four colours so that the patterns do not become a jumble. Use the same few motifs on all the pieces of furniture and soft furnishings that you intend to paint, picking up on a design feature already present somewhere in the room and.)

Using the same motifs, four delicate garlands linked by graceful ribbons were traced and painted with fabric paints (see

4. Chrysanthemum flower-heads were painted at the top of the frame of the swing mirror, while the design on the lampshade exactly matches that of the chair seat cover.

page 134) on the chair seat. The pink piping around the cushion acts as a frame for the design and links the seat to the edging on the ties and pelmet of the curtain. To do this yourself, work up your design on paper first. When you are happy with it, copy it on to the fabric with tailors' chalk. Alternatively, trace the design on to tracing paper and transfer it to the fabric in the usual way. Make sure the material is taut, then pin the tracing paper and the waxless carbon paper in place. Once the design has been transferred, paint the motifs one colour at a time and fix by covering the material with a cloth and iron smoothly over the top (according to the manufacturer's instructions), being careful not to smudge your design.

The same motifs were painted on the drawers, cupboard doors and top of the dressing table to create symmetrical patterns (as shown in photographs 3 and 4).

The ribbon motif provides the frame for the large, central pink rose painted on the doors, and a pink border, or beading, has been used to frame the panels. The handles of the doors and drawers were also painted pink to finish the effect.

Framing motifs and patterns is a useful way to set them off by drawing attention to them and 'fixing' them in place. In addition, if you use the same colour to frame motifs on various different pieces, it will help to link them, making a more cohesive overall design. Painting beading is painstaking work. The best way to do this is to mask off either side of the area to be beaded with low-tack masking tape so that you can achieve a clean edge when painting, even with the unsteadiest of hands.

The motifs painted on the swing mirror and drawer complement those painted on the dressing table and lampshade, their inspiration clearly visible in the mirror, which reflects the rich floral patterning of the curtains (as shown in photograph 4).

This time the flowing ribbon apparent on all the pieces was painted pink to match the actual ribbon decorating the crenellated lampshade on the right.

High up on the wall, the whatnot with turned supports and curved shelves and back was edged with pink to define the shelves and link it with the pink details and edgings featured on the rest of the painted furniture (as shown in photograph 5). An enchanting 'fun' detail was painted at each end of the back of the whatnot. The small figure of a squirrel was transferred in the usual way using tracing paper and super-charged waxless carbon paper and then painted one colour at a time, finishing with a dark outline so that the figure was not 'lost' so high up the wall. The squirrel is actually pointing at the bottom of the ribbon decoration on the wall, and although of a completely different scale, it seems to be a part of the same scene as the stencilled dragonfly painted in delicate pink and blue just to its right on the wall.

5. Although decorated in the same colours, the whatnot features a different – still naturalistic – motif that links it to the wall above.

PRE-TEENS: Basic Room

By pre-teens, apart from the bunk bed, which is still in place, a number of changes have taken place. A small table has been incorporated into the basic desk unit installed in early school-age to make room for a home computer or a small television, and an extra pinboard fixed in place on the other side of the window for more certificates, notes and postcards. The shelving to the left of the desk now provides space for large-sized textbooks as well as light relief in the form of a music system. To accommodate visitors, large sag bags have been placed on the floor in one corner and the ever-useful toybox transformed into a small table for this area. This is also an ideal place to relax in, read a book or listen to music, as distinct from the workmanlike desk unit. Other new additions include a swing mirror on he chest of drawers, and softer, more adult curtains to frame the window instead of a roller blind.

BASIC REQUIREMENTS

Space may well be a problem by the time your child reaches this age, especially if he or she has to share a room with another child. Your ingenuity will certainly be put to the test when you are trying to create enough storage and work space, not to mention bed space, for two children. Whether one or two children use the room, reorganizing the work area may well be the biggest priority. Two work surfaces will probably be needed—one for a personal computer if your child has one, and another for homework and hobbies.

Breaking the level

Now is a good time to accommodate a study area in addition to a play area and a sleep area. If the room is large enough, it is a good idea to create three identifiably different areas that reflect the three different activities.

Try introducing different levels into the room to help define the separate areas and make the room more interesting. Make a broad step in front of the window, for example, with a hard-wearing rug on top, and position a desk with drawers, plus a chair. Light will shine on to the desk during the day, and your child will feel that he or she is entering a different zone as he or she steps up to the desk.

Add a desk lamp for evening homework —a central light is unlikely to be sufficient, especially if your child has his or her back to it. Erect shelves on the wall to one side of the window, or place a freestanding bookshelf unit to one or both sides of the desk for books and ornaments.

The play area might be adjacent to the work area, but at the lower level. Your child will probably have outgrown any small table and chairs, so remove them and make the space into more of a leisure area. Arrange colourful sag bags along the wall, or bunch them in a corner to provide a distinct sitting area. Carpet this and the

Below: the work area in this room is very clearly defined and cosy. Sandwiched between two freestanding bookshelves, the roll-top desk and chair were first stippled (see page 146) in pastel blue and then decorated with floral and ribbon motifs. Also stippled in pastel blue, the bookshelf columns store a large number of books and records.

sleeping area in, for example, a short-pile mottled carpet that is still hard-wearing and conceals stains effectively but which gives a more sophisticated feel.

Developing the work area

If you have not already incorporated a desk or table into the room, and if the room is large enough, now is a good time to acquire a proper desk with drawers and a good-quality, adjustable chair that will give lengthy service. A matching table set at right angles to the desk, or alongside it, is always useful. Alternatively, using a scaffolding system, build an all-in-one shelving and desk unit against a wall. Such units have the advantage that you can take them down and reassemble them in a different way, perhaps using extra pieces, as your child's requirements change.

Another essential is an adjustable desk lamp. If you don't like the colours available, you could paint one yourself with enamel paints to blend or contrast with the decorative scheme of the room. Jolly up the desk with novelty items that are functional, such as a bright red 1950s-looking letter rack, a pencil box with your child's favourite characters painted on it, a large block of multi-coloured notepaper—the list is endless. Let your child choose the things that appeal to him or her.

Ingenious storage suggestions

If you haven't already done so, install fitted cupboards or a pair of freestanding wardrobes—complete with a full-length mirror, as your child will probably now be taking an interest in his or her appearance—to hold all your child's clothes. Your child is likely to have acquired any number of cumbersome possessions, such as an extensive railway set, a musical instrument such as a guitar, and a range of board games. By now the size of the individual items belonging to your child and the quantity of them mean a simple toybox is far from adequate. So, if you have not already done so, you will need to put up a storage system of some sort. Flexible shelving with vertical dividers is a good solution. Perhaps you could extend a system already in existence by taking the shelving right up to the ceiling.

If your child is keen on trains or racing cars and has a large set taking up valuable space, you could construct a movable platform for it, using pulleys and a winch to store it at ceiling level when not in use. Use a sound, square piece of wood for this, on which the track and landscape can be permanently left in place. Make sure too that the system is absolutely safe, and always be there to supervise the winching up or down.

Below: in this small bedroom, the built-in, floor-to-ceiling cupboards provide storage space for a large number of clothes, sports gear and toys. To make maximum use of the space, the cupboards were also fitted with bright red 'grids' attached to the walls.

Left: this room gives the appearance of being spacious while also being extremely well equipped. Desk and wardrobe – both painted white with spots of bright red on the handles – are fitted into the alcove, which also contains open shelving for toys, books and a lamp. On the opposite side of the room, a red trolley fitted with white-painted wire baskets provides a useful movable storage system.

Sleeping and relaxing

A bed or, if the room is shared, two beds or bunk beds, are obvious essentials, preferably fitted with drawers underneath for extra storage. If the room is being shared, you might find it a more efficient use of space to put together or buy a specially designed modular sleeping and study unit in which one of the beds is raised and work surfaces are incorporated into the system, stabilizing the tubular frame.

Make sure that there are shelves in the bedside table for more books. Breakages and spillages are less likely to be a feature of life by now, so you could fit a carpet if it's time for the floor surface to be renewed, although it is wise to stick with short-pile carpet as deep-pile carpeting is still not a very practical choice.

Your child is likely to want to invite his or her friends into his room to play, chat, or do some homework together, so introduce more seating, either in the form of reasonably comfortable chairs (director's chairs that fold away are good value and save on space) or large sag bags and cushions, depending on the style of the room. You might also like to change the lighting scheme. Install more wall-mounted uplighters for a diffused effect, and complement them with task lights. For example, an adjustable reading light on the desk and beside the bed, and a spot light fixed on the bookshelves or storage system and trained on the sag bags, where your child is likely to sit and read.

Children of this age often like to cover the walls with posters and postcards. Even if your child uses a re-usable adhesive such as Blu-tack for this purpose, it may still pull small chips of paint or paper off when the poster is removed. If you want to avoid marring the paint effect or wallpaper, put up several pinboards all around the room (you can cut these into interesting shapes such as clouds or half-moons if you want to make them a feature of the room) for pictures. Alternatively, put up a picture rail that will take drawing pins, or fix a group of cork tiles to the door or one area of wall.

TEENAGERS 13 PLUS

Rooms for teenagers are often the most challenging to design and decorate simply because they are usually required to serve so many different functions: not just as a bedroom, but also a study, a place to relax in and a room in which to entertain friends. If your teenager's room is large enough, you could treat it almost like a bedsit or studio flat, with the furniture and fittings cleverly arranged in such a way that they provide three core areas: bedroom, study and leisure area. To stop the room looking cluttered and overcrowded, keep the colour scheme fairly simple and light, although you could use slightly different paint treatments or wallpaper in each area to differentiate them, or divide the room up into different levels using raised platforms. And coordinating curtains, bed linen, upholstery and so on will pull the various elements into a cohesive decorative scheme. However, it is not always possible for one room to serve all these requirements; if your teenager's room is small, no matter how ingenious you are, cramming everything in will only result in a cramped, overbearing look. Indeed, not all teenagers want their bedrooms to be anything but bedrooms, and there is something to be said for providing a separate room, or at least a quiet area, elsewhere in the house for doing homework and studying, if space permits.

As for pre-teens, the following pages can cover only a selected range of rooms that have been specially designed for (and sometimes by) teenagers. You may find that there is no one scheme that really appeals to you and your teenager, but elements that do. In which case, there is nothing stopping you from using these as a starting point to designing your own scheme; and, if you need further inspiration, look at the objects around you—a favourite poster, for example, or a painting, or a beautiful piece of fabric. They may well suggest the general colour scheme and approach you would feel happy with.

DECORATING IDEAS

Teenagers tend to have very firm ideas about the sort of decoration they want in their rooms, and they may well be keen to do the job themselves. Their tastes are bound to be more sophisticated now, although many may want to experiment with different looks and less orthodox effects to put the stamp of their individuality on the room. Talk through all the possibilities with your teenager and try not to dampen his or her enthusiasm to experiment with different decorative effects: they may turn out to be stunning.

Usually, the main challenge when designing for this age group is to create three easily identifiable areas in the one room: the sleeping area, the work area and the leisure area.

Decorating the sleeping area

In a fairly large room you could try a wall finish such as ragging or rag-rolling (see page 148). Then, in the sleeping area, give fitted cupboards the same treatment so that they blend with the walls. If your teenager prefers a more subtle finish on the walls, you could restrict rag-rolling to the panels of doors and cupboards, perhaps dragging the surrounds and lining the panels to define them further. You might also like to rag-roll the bedhead and footboard to tie them in with the cupboards. Whatever paint finish you and your teenager decide on for the walls, you could continue the same technique over the radiators to camouflage them. Of course, you might prefer to hang wallpaper, es-

Page 106: in this bright, elegant interior, stencilled motifs executed in shades of silver, grey and black have been employed to coordinate the soft furnishings with the furniture. This helps to minimize any sense of clutter (often a problem in a teenager's room!) and contributes to the visual sense of space – an effect that is accentuated by carrying the pastel grey sponged finish over the walls and wardrobe.

Right: the pleated pastel pink fabric embellishing the four-poster, dressing table and window, and echoed in the stencilled motifs decorating the pastel green bedside and sofa tables, lends this bedroom a decidedly feminine air.

pecially in the sleeping area, in which you might want to create, for example, a relaxing English cottage bedroom look. If so, try dragging, stippling or sponging (see pages 143, 146 and 142) the skirting board and furniture—bedside table, chest of drawers, wardrobe—in a colour that complements the main colour of the cottage print. Copy the motif from the wallpaper and stencil it on the bed cover and pillowcases together to link these elements.

If the sleeping area is on the same level as the leisure area, it is possible to divide the two with a folding screen. Stencil the cottage print on the bedroom side of the screen and paint the leisure side in a colour and style that complements the

decorative scheme there. Alternatively, you could divide the two areas with bookshelves and a storage system for records and tapes. Make such a divider seem appropriate to the sleeping area by painting it in the same style and colour as the rest of the 'bedroom' furniture.

Identifying the work area

However small the room, make sure that the work area is clearly defined and decorated in a style conducive to study. You could, for example, recarpet it in workmanlike grey. Then, for a metallic, hi-tech look, paint the desk with grey Hammerite paint (see page 133). Make sure the desk is well lit, either by spotlights from above or with

Above: this attic room has been furnished to serve as both a study and a bedroom. Whilst the arrangement of the furniture creates clearly defined areas for sleeping and studying, pastel orange-pinks, blues and yellows are employed throughout to coordinate the décor. Note how the large, framed wall mirror behind the desk is used to create the illusion of a greater sense of space and light – a particularly useful trick in any confined area.

Above: although a bedroom, the emphasis in this modern, spacious interior is clearly on study – the functional single bed appears almost as a reluctant concession to sleep when set against the simple table, fitted bookcase and mobile filing cabinet. Pastel greys and greens provide a quietly stimulating (though not distracting) backdrop for work; whilst primary reds, yellows and blues are used with discretion to strike a youthful, energetic note.

a desk lamp—a black halogen lamp would be the most suitable for the hi-tech style.

Your teenager might well prefer, however, an antique look for the room, in which case a faded canvas rug would be more suited to the work area. Paint a border on the rug, using stencils (see pages 138–41), blocks (see pages 74–5) or transfers (see pages 70–1) and dusky colours. If the desk is of poor quality wood, you could try wood-graining it for a high quality antique look, although this does require a certain amount of skill and confidence. Copy the grain of the wood you wish to emulate—rosewood, walnut or oak are all good choices. For a more 'country' look, try the dragging tech-

nique (see page 143), or stippling (see page 146) on the desk, in a pastel shade. In all these cases, extend the paint finish to the desk chair.

If you have placed the desk immediately in front of the window, make sure that the curtains or blinds complement both the desk area and the rest of the room. And if you do locate the desk area against a wall without a window, try to make certain that your teenager does not sit with his or her back to daylight. Paint the wall a shade that is easy on the eye, and use one of the more subtle paint effects, such as colour-washing (see page 147), sponging (see page 142) or stippling, which creates an interesting texture (see page 146). And, where possible, fix a pinboard above the desk for notes and messages.

Decorating the leisure area

For the leisure area, either fit the same carpet or one that tones in with the canvas rug or carpet in the study area—unless, of course, you are able to screen out that part of the room entirely. Alternatively, stain the floorboards and place a rug in the centre—try an Omega or 1930s design. For a hi-tech finish you could leave the floorboards uncovered, painting them black with hard-wearing yacht paint.

A futon placed in this area, whether for the occupant to use as both bed and sofa,

or for a friend to stay the night, might be useful and could suggest a Japanese minimalist style for the rest of the décor. Use neutral tones—say, cream and light-grey cushions and mattress—set against a black floor or futon base. Grey-sponged table lamps look good on the low side tables. And tall uplighters help to provide more diffused lighting. Try to use only localized light sources in the room: these will help define areas and create interesting shadows.

If your teenager has a hi-fi and television, place them at the edges of the area to help define it and to keep a reasonable proportion of free central floor space on which to place a low coffee table and

Left: in this young teenager's bedroom, a simple plasterboard and stud wall construction has been furnished as an alcove sleeping area. Illuminated by recessed lighting, which doesn't intrude into the limited space, this 'compartment' appears almost as a room within a room – clearly separated from the study area, which is sited directly beneath the large window bay. Building a desk around the bay provides a spacious worksurface, and takes maximum advantage of the natural light; sensibly, venetian blinds have been installed to deflect direct sunlight. Although a number of strongly contrasting colours have been chosen throughout, the striped pattern that runs over most of the surfaces unites them all in a cohesive and attractive whole.

Above: in this striking
bedroom, pale apricot and
white striped walls, a white
venetian blind and a
beechwood floor were chosen
to provide a subtle backdrop to
an eclectic collection of
furnishings and decorative
objects. Highly collectable
(and expensive) tinplate toys
are combined with enlarged
photocopies of classical
mosaics, terracotta wall lights
and high-backed chairs, to
create a sophisticated interior.

several large cushions. A Japanese screen
on another edge, perhaps between the desk
area and leisure area, would be in keeping.
Alternatively, some freestanding black- or
grey-painted shelves would also act as a
divider and provide storage space for books
and records and tapes as well.

For a more jazzy look, try painting the
floorboards in a rich colour, such as jade,
and installing wooden slatted chairs and a
tubular sofa bed painted in contrasting bold
colours. Paint a bright abstract design on
the bed linen, if it is plain, using fabric
paints or crayons (see page 134) in all the
colours you have used so far. Use the same

design and colours on the cushions and
perhaps on the curtains as well.

A fireplace or a piece of furniture can
make a strong focal point in the leisure
area of the room, and might well be the
starting point when you are establishing
the tone and atmosphere of this area.
Sponge, drag, or stencil it for a rustic
look—keeping the pattern simple—or try
painting shapes and figures on the mantelpiece and down the sides of the fireplace. If
you wish to do this, make sure that there is
more freehand painting in the room: a
screen would be ideal for a similar treatment, as would cupboard doors.

MURALS

The most sophisticated type of mural it is possible to paint is *trompe l'oeil*—a mural that deceives the eye into thinking it is looking at a real object or scene rather than a representation of one. To paint such a mural you must understand how to create perspective, using light and shade (see pages 154–5). The easiest way to start is to copy from real life and to compare the painting continually with the real subject.

A popular *trompe-l'oeil* mural is a view of a window with an interesting vista beyond. Such a painting can make the room appear larger and lighter, while at the same time providing, perhaps, a much more pleasant view than that which actually lies beyond the wall. To give the view perspective, paint something in the foreground—an ornament on the windowsill, or a cat looking out of the window, for example.

Left: in this palatial interior, the archway that connects a somewhat spartan play area with the bedroom beyond, has been dramatically embellished with *trompe-l'oeil* pillars and Egyptian motifs. The illusion of three-dimensionality is achieved by sponging different tones of sand and beige coloured glazes within the outlines of the pillars, to simulate areas of light and shade (see pages 154–5). By applying the same stencilled motif above the arch and the window beyond; by decorating the chest with the stencilled figures used around the wall, and by stencilling hieroglyphics on the window blind, the Egyptian theme has been cleverly used to unite the two rooms on either side of the large archway.

Left: although this mural was painted on stretched canvas to fit the window frame, a similar scene could be painted on a blind using fabric paints (see page 134).

Below left: sophisticated *trompe-l'oeil* techniques have been employed to transform a flat wall surface into a seemingly three-dimensional curved niche. Displaying an elegant vase on a marbled plinth, it is surrounded by *trompe-l'oeil* shelving, books and decorative objects. Note the little man, painted in to 'support' the very real light switch! *Trompe-l'oeil* work of this kind can be used to add visual interest to otherwise architecturally bland areas.

Another *trompe-l'oeil* mural that creates the illusion of space is the image of an open door, leading down a long passageway; or that of a window through which you can see another room. A three-dimensional image of an illusory bedside lamp on an illusory bedside table, set against the wall in a dark corner, will make the room seem brighter—as will a realistic painting of a flower arrangement on a chest of drawers.

Trompe l'oeil painting can improve the look of a room, or make an out-of-place element seem a part of the theme. For example, melamine fitted cupboards would look wrong in a country house room, but paint illusory swathes of rich fabric over them and they are transformed into a feature in keeping with the décor.

Opposite page: if you can't afford a swimming pool in the back garden for the children, here is the next best thing. This landscape mural of manicured gardens and the countryside beyond, framed by the generous pleats of *trompe-l'oeil* Regency striped curtains, would make a dramatic and seemingly spacious addition to a teenager's room – and should certainly impress his or her friends!

CONTEMPORARY IDEAS

Most teenagers are anxious to assert their independence and to be considered adult. They are therefore likely to want to entertain their friends in their own room rather than in the family living room. Consequently, a teenager's room should reflect character in its decoration.

Although the decorative ideas outlined in this section were devised as complete looks, this does not mean that individual elements of them cannot be applied on their own—much depends on the amount of time, money and energy you and your teenager have to hand.

Stark lines

Perhaps your teenager is a great fan of the Modernists, in love with starkness and straight lines. To achieve such a look clutter must be banished, so there should be plenty of storage space in the room. Fitted cupboards are best, so that most of the belongings can be put out of sight. If

possible, push all the furniture out to the edges of the room to leave a large, empty space in the centre. Then paint everything a pale colour, such as white or off-white.

Colourwash (see page 147) the walls and fitted cupboards for a cohesive look; wash or stain the floorboards white, and wash freestanding pieces of furniture white. Next, introduce flat lines accentuated in strong colours, such as black, red or blue. Paint a large geometric shape (or shapes) on one wall; line the drawers of a chest and the panels of the cupboards; pick out the tops of the legs of the bed and chairs. And finally, introduce another strong colour, such as yellow or orange, into the geometric pattern and on to door and drawer handles.

An additional idea, in keeping with the style, would be to paint or stencil a similar geometric pattern similar to that painted on the wall, on to the bed cover. Then reverse the colours, but keep the same design, on the pillowcases or cushions. Do not, however, stray from geometrics and the colours you've already used, or the effect will be ruined.

Sweeping lines and rich colour

Your teenager may love the broad, fluid brush strokes and warm colours of Matisse, in which case you will probably need to sponge (see page 142) or stipple (see page 146) the walls in two or three similar toned pastel shades for a textured finish. Sponge or drag (see pages 142 and 143) the pieces of furniture to match the walls and each other, and perhaps strip the floorboards either leaving them bare, or staining them a very pale pastel colour to complement the rest of the décor.

Then introduce large, curving lines and irregular circles in soft reds, greens and

Below: numerous pastel colours have been combined to embellish the simple lines of the furniture and soft furnishings in this bright and cheerful teenager's bed-sitting room. Pale green colourwashed walls (see page 147) provide a complementary and unobtrusive backdrop that contributes to the sense of spaciousness.

Left: this teenager's room has been furnished and decorated on functional lines – and no less aesthetically pleasing for that. Plenty of shelving and storage space ensure clothing, books and general clutter can be neatly put away. The clean lines of the furniture also encourage tidiness, whilst the plain off-white walls provide a suitable backcloth for a small collection of posters.

Below: in the study area of this teenage bedroom, cheap MDF (medium density fibreboard) has been decorated with a dramatic silver and blue spatter finish (see page 145), and arranged to form a functional and attractive L-shaped work station.

yellows over the whole drop of the curtains and the bed cover. You might also make swirling shapes snake their way across the pillows and along the tops and bottoms of cupboards and chests of drawers.

But for a more ambitious scheme, why not try your hand at a triumphant Impressionist or Post-Impressionist mural on the wall. If you do embark on such a large, atmospheric mural, don't overdo the amount of pattern on the furniture, or the scheme will look too busy and the eye will be distracted from the walls.

Chic finishes

For an elegant look, try ragging or rag-rolling (see page 148) the walls in deep, luxuriant blues or greens. Continue with the same technique over the fitted cupboards too, if the room contains them: either rag every inch of them or restrict the effect to the panels, and drag all around

tack masking tape placed ½–1 in (1–3 cm) in from the edge of the piece you want to line (this creates an edge lining). Using a ½-in (1.2-cm) standard decorators' brush, apply the paint to the masked-off edges. Then carefully remove the masking tape. To create a fine line, use a ruler and an indelible felt-tip pen. Position the ruler at the required distance from, and parallel to, the edge. Then mark out the fine lines with the pen—waiting for each to dry before repositioning the ruler for the next one. If the ink has crept under the ruler, remove it with a cotton-wool bud moistened with white spirit.

Exotic influences

Your teeenager may prefer the room to have the exotic flavour of distant lands. You could give the room an Arabian flavour by incorporating stencilled arabesques (a highly decorative scrolled or interlaced regular pattern based on, but hardly recognizable as, a plant form) in a border around the walls and in decorative panels on the bedhead, footboard, on the wardrobe, and on the panels of a screen (to separate areas of the room, perhaps). Or, if your teenager prefers something more realistic, use stylized leaves or flowers to provide interesting borders. You could repeat such motifs on the lampshades and even cushions. An Arabian-style rug placed in the centre of the floor or hung like a tapestry would also contribute to the atmosphere.

For a Far Eastern look try to incorporate elements of the delicate chinoiserie designs traditionally painted on porcelain, lacquerware and screens. Copy the motifs from real examples (or from books about antiques) and paint them on the smaller elements in the room, such as lamp holders and lampshades, mirror frames and clocks. Paint stylized, naturalistic scenes on the wardrobe panels or screen, or perhaps on the curtains or blinds and the bed cover.

Above: this elegant, and expensive looking, window covering is in fact a cheap roller blind that has been reversed-stencilled with an unusual bow motif. Strips of low-tack masking were positioned on the surface, the blind was then sprayed with black car spray paint, and the tape was finally removed. (It is important to protect eyes, nose and mouth, and to ensure good ventilation in the work area, when spraying with cellulose-based paints.)

them, both vertically and horizontally. Drag, comb or spatter (see pages 143, 145 and 144) the furniture in the same rich, deep tones, then line drawers and panels in a complementary shade of the same colour. Pick out handles in this complementary shade too, and consider fantasy marbling both decorative and functional objects.

For more textured effects, try sponging or fine spraying (see pages 142 and 145) the fabrics in the room, using the same tones. And line the edges of the duvet cover or bedspread, and the pillowcases and cushion covers as a border.

Lining

A combed finish on furniture looks very elegant, or you might like to line the pieces to define their contours. The easiest way to do this is to mark out the line using low-

An even more exotic and very effective idea is to cover the walls with fabric. Dress fabric is ideal because it is cheap compared to special wall fabrics, and the range of designs is much wider (if you want extra insulation, back the fabric first with cotton or polyester thickening, which comes in rolls up to 6 ft 8 in [2 m] wide). For an exotic ambience, choose a suitably oriental-looking design in the appropriate colours. Other fabrics that can be used include cheesecloth, muslin, Indian cotton quilts, and artists' canvas. (If you are feeling ambitious, paint your own design using fabric paints, see page 134).

There are a number of ways to fix fabric to the wall: using adhesive, a staple gun or a special wall-track system. When using adhesive, it is best to use a non-stretch, fade-resistant fabric. And remember to apply the paste to the wall and not to the fabric. Or use a staple gun to fix the fabric directly on to the wall (use this method if you have backed it with another fabric first), making sure that you overlap the pieces as you go along. Cover any frayed edges or staples with braiding.

Another method you might consider is a wall-track system, which basically provides a frame into which the fabric is fixed (this consists of a long plastic strip with 'jaws' which conceal untidy edges, an adhesive strip which holds the fabric in place, together with a special tool to push the fabric into the frame). The strips should be screwed to the top and bottom of the walls (just above the skirting) and then the fabric secured in position. The advantages of such a system are that the fabric can be re-moved to be cleaned from time to time (do make sure you have chosen a fabric that won't shrink) and you can also change the fabric for a new one to completely trans-form the entire look of the room.

Whatever fabric you use, be sure to treat it with a flame retardant spray!

Above: this exotic attic bedroom has been given an air of adult sophistication by ingenious use of delicate fabric, stencilled decoration and concealed lighting. The trailing vine border, echoing the wall basket and canopy tiebacks, has been applied with discretion – leaving the bedspread undecorated is a nicely understated touch.

Left: the other end of this tranquil bedroom serves as an area for reading and relaxing – stencilled cushions provide the informal seating.

PROJECT FIVE
A
CONTEMPORARY
ROOM

The modern, hi-tech appearance of this spacious, high-ceilinged room was created by painting some of the furniture in a metallic finish paint (see page 133) and a choice of black and grey eggshell. Chrome furniture also contributes to the overall look. The walls were roughly colourwashed (see page 147) in pale blue and white vinyl matt emulsion to provide a perfect foil for the black and dark greys of the furniture and the vertically striped carpet.

Although the bed is centrally placed, clearly indicating that this is a bedroom, the room has been cleverly designed to function as a study and sitting room as well, mainly due to the simplicity of its layout combined with a carefully structured colour scheme. Although not clearly shown here, the near corner houses a solid desk and chair for studying and homework, with shelving above. To change the mood in the evening, uplighters were chosen for either side of the bed to introduce a softer, glowing light, while the Saturn-style lamp in the ceiling is an unusual and eye-catching item that produces a diffused central light.

In keeping with the uncluttered look, curtains were discarded in favour of smart, dark blue metal venetian blinds that complement the strongly linear quality of the décor. These were also chosen to offset the surrounding woodwork painted in mid-grey, which matches the spattered skirting board and cornice.

The finely striped dark grey and white carpeting is complemented by a large rug

1. Colourwashed and veined walls are framed by a mid-grey painted cornice and skirting board with a spattered black, red and blue finish.

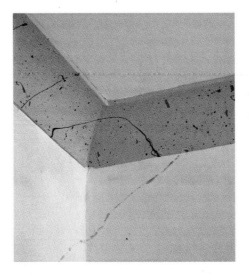

placed off-centre, and the black-and-white abstract bed linen introduces further discreet patterning into the room.

The walls were first painted in white vinyl matt emulsion, and then unevenly colourwashed (see page 147) in blue and white vinyl matt emulsion to give a slightly mottled appearance. When the paint was dry, veins of blue-grey were painted sparsely around the room using a small round artists' brush, and highlighted with white, to give the merest suggestion of marbling. Trying to imitate the real thing requires considerable skill – and dedication if you decide to cover such a large area! An

2. The dark-grey painted and white veined console table stands out against the pale wall and is the perfect table for a chrome lamp.

3. The grey ragged stripes give this white wardrobe a distinctive, luxuriant look. The high-tech look of chrome trolley next to it is ideally suited to its use as a TV and video stand.

interesting variation is to use unusual colours and veining to create a fantasy marble finish that does not exist in nature, and is less exacting to execute. The cornice and skirting board were then painted mid-grey to frame the wall and to link it to the overall scheme (as shown in photograph 1).

It was decided at this stage, however, that they looked too solid, even though the colour was right. The solution was to spatter them in black, dark blue and wine red to break the colour up and introduce a more lively note. Unlike the spattering shown on page 145, this was achieved using the end of a small, round stick (the end of a small paint brush would do) and a very slightly diluted mixture of eggshell paint with white spirit (don't make the

mixture too thin or the spatters will run).

Spattering is a messy business, so do make sure that the carpet is covered with a large piece of old sheeting, and that you are wearing old clothes. To protect the wall, take a large sheet of paper and stick it in place with low-tack masking tape at the place where you are going to start working, moving it as you work along. Also have to hand some clean, old rags and white spirit to quickly mop up any drips or accidents.

Dip the end of the stick into the first diluted eggshell paint mixture and flick the paint on to the surface with a brisk wrist action. Don't overload the stick with too much paint, otherwise the spatters will run, particularly when working on an up-right surface. To vary the direction of the

4. Special metallic paint can be bought to create both a hammered or smooth finish depending on your preference. The metallic finish has a close affinity to the chrome handles.

spattering, flick the paint from different distances and angles. Work along the skirting board and cornice with one colour only and allow it to dry before starting on the next colour to ensure that each spattered colour is clean and distinct. Remember to thoroughly clean the end of the stick with a cloth and white spirit before starting on the next colour.

The console table is a purely decorative item here. Found in a dilapidated state, it has been given a new lease of life by painting it in dark-grey eggshell. When the paint was dry, white veining was added with a fine brush to echo that on the wall (as shown in photograph 2 on page 122). To protect such a finish, cover it in one or two coats of flat or eggshell, wax-free varnish (see page 133), although with an eggshell finish this is probably unnecessary unless it is likely to experience a lot of wear and tear. The inexpensive metallic table lamp completes the transformation, providing a warm pool of light in this corner of the room in the evening.

The curves on the wall mirror were cleverly picked up by the unusual black, geometric shape painted at the top of the white and grey wardrobe (as shown in photograph 3 on page 123). A fairly ordinary piece, it has been lent interest by ragging (see page 148) three vertical stripes in grey across the doors. The lines were carefully pencilled in first using a metre rule and then wide strips of low-tack masking tape applied to either side of the bands to ensure a clean line when ragging. The result is a highly textured finish that also suggests the pattern of marble.

The low cupboard, which provides invaluable storage space for sports equipment and games, was painted with a metallic finish paint (see page 133) to give it a pitted sheen, linking it with the chrome items elsewhere in the room (as shown in photograph 4). This provides a tough, attractive surface that can withstand knocks and bumps, and should retain its smart appearance for many years to come.

Finally, the open chrome and glass shelving unit (as shown in photograph 5) is perfectly sited in the living room area, and gives its occupant the opportunity to display his fine collection of fifties' toys and artefacts, as well as well-thumbed copies of childhood annuals.

5. This chrome bookshelf features the archetypical curves of the fifties, also evidenced in the models of classic cars displayed on the glass shelves.

TEENAGERS: Basic Room

In this teenager's room, the bunk bed has now been discarded in favour of a single bed that doubles as a settee during the day, with large, firm cushions providing a comfortable backrest. This could equally be a stacking bed as shown in the toddlers' section (see page 55) to cater for a friend staying overnight, or a sofa bed. A sag-bag provides additional seating, and the toybox now serves as a proper coffee table, while still functioning as a useful storage place. A small side table and lamp have also been introduced into the room and placed beside the bed/settee. Here, the lamp helps to create a softer light conducive to this seating area, and at the same time serves as a bedside light. Instead of toys and picture books, the shelves now house a hi-fi system and a large record and cassette collection; any noise problem is considerably reduced by the introduction of wall-to-wall thick carpeting!

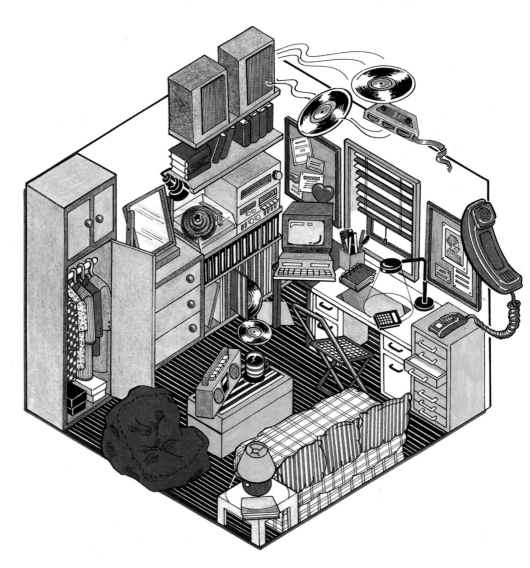

BASIC REQUIREMENTS

Designing rooms for teenagers requires the most ingenuity, for the requirements of teenagers are many and varied. The room must act as a bedroom, although it will probably be used more as a living room, so it must have extra comfortable seating and probably space for a hi-fi and records, cassettes, and a television. In addition, the room will probably serve as a study (unless, of course, a quiet place is provided elsewhere in the house), so space must be made for a desk and bookshelves.

Making the most of the space

If the room is large enough to contain three distinct areas, each serving a different function, then you can create the perfect teenage room. More often than not, though, space is a problem. If this is the case, you might like to have a platform built for the bed, if the ceiling is high enough, to free some floor space underneath. You can buy these ready-made in steel tubing, or get your local carpenter to install a wooden frame. The area underneath can then be used to house a wardrobe, chest of drawers and dressing table, or be kitted out as a cosy study area; in effect introducing another storey to the room.

You can easily transform a floor-level bed into a settee during the daytime by throwing over an attractive, hard-wearing cover and lots of scatter cushions. Alternatively, replace the bed with a sofa bed—a

Below: two young teenagers share this bedroom, and the furniture has been arranged to provide adequate sleeping, studying and storage areas, whilst making the maximum use of the limited space. By colour matching the walls to the fitted shelving and units, the latter are made less obtrusive; the combination of primary reds and blues in the soft furnishings introduce a brighter note.

Below right: this elegant teenager's room features wall-length built-in cupboards, with padded doors covered in the same material as the curtains. Clutter is easily kept to a minimum, with the added advantage that the units provide effective soundproofing.

Below: the fitted storage and shelving unit has been finished in the same two-tone blue striped paint finish as the surrounding walls. In confined spaces, this is a good way of making large items of furniture 'recede' into the background.

futon also serves both purposes—and cover it with cushions during the day. Place large cushions or sag bags on the floor around it to create a leisure area, and set the hi-fi and/or television on low tables or in a single shelving unit. If there is space, include a coffee table in this area of the room (an old trunk or even an upturned tea chest painted or covered with a glued-on fabric will serve); and illuminate with diffused uplighters, or spotlights set at interesting angles, to create atmospheric shadows.

Entertaining and working facilities

Your teenager will probably need more privacy now that he or she no longer considers him or herself a child. Having their own wash basin acknowledges this development and is useful if a friend comes to stay overnight, and also so that a kettle can be filled (provided the cold tap is connected to the rising main). It might also be useful to provide a low table with a

wipeable surface on which to stand the kettle and make tea.

Set the work area of the room apart, if possible, by partitioning it off with a screen (solid, freestanding shelving units can also act as screens, while offering useful library space) or placing the desk on a platform. Your teenager will probably require many bookshelves in this area, and possibly also a filing cabinet. Make sure that you provide a good localized task light for the desk, preferably a light that can be angled, and that the chair is firm and gives proper support for the back. You might also need to put an additional table in this area, on which to stand a word processor or home computer or a typewriter.

Reducing noise levels

One problem you may have to contend with where teenagers are concerned, is noise. Your teenager may like to play records and tapes very loudly. If this is the case, tell them to turn it down! Failing these, try

soundproofing the walls to some extent by covering them with egg crates. These provide an interesting, textured wall that your teenager may love, especially when it is painted. If not, simply cover the egg crates with plasterboard and then decorate like a regular wall. The alternative is to sound-proof the room properly: to insulate the floor put insulating board directly on top of the floorboards, followed by hardboard, then the carpet, vinyl cork or tiled flooring. If you want to insulate the walls, do this before deciding on a finish. First remove skirtings and electrical fittings. Then place a layer of plasterboard over the existing wall finish, or, for extra insulation, place new plasterboard on battens and fill the space with a layer of insulating material (like loft insulation). This cuts noise coming in from outside the room and noise from inside travelling out.

Hanging rugs on the walls will also help to muffle sound and can look very attractive. Indian cotton dhurries are relatively inexpensive and come in many individual styles. And you could try making a canopy roof, using striped material, to absorb sound and provide an intriguing ceiling. To do this, first position battening all the way around the room at picture-rail height. Then measure from the centre point of the ceiling to one corner of the battening, and from the centre point to the corner next to it. Cut out a triangle of fabric to this measurement. Repeat for the other three sides of the room. Pin, tack and stitch the four triangles of fabric together, and hem the outer edges. Measure between the joists in the ceiling and cut out a piece of plywood to this size. Cut a hole in the centre large enough to hold the light flex and the fabric. Push the raw edges of the centre of the fabric through the hole and secure with fabric adhesive or staples. Screw the plywood into place on the ceiling—into the joists behind. Refix the ceiling rose over the hole and replace the light. Pull the fabric taut at the edges and tack on to wooden battening. Conceal the join with the picture rail or with pretty braiding.

Above: in this older teenager's bedroom an area in front of the window has been set aside for study. The efficient-looking black desk is elegantly contrasted with a matching Pacific blue angled desk lamp and venetian blind, whilst the pastel-coloured geometric shapes stencilled tumbling from the softly diffused light source are employed to add a note of design-conscious frivolity.

MATERIALS AND TECHNIQUES

The previous chapters of this book have revealed the enormous diversity of paint effects you can create on plaster, wood, fabric and metal, and have given you some ideas on how to use them to make the most of a child's room, whatever the age. This chapter looks in more detail at carrying out some of the paint techniques shown and addresses the problem of achieving a good painting surface.

At first glance, the list of tools and materials here may seem lengthy. However, you do not need to amass all of them at once. Rather, decide on the work you need to do in the room you are decorating—including preparation —and then purchase only the appropriate tools. However, it is a mistake to skimp on either the range of tools required or the quality of them. If possible buy sable brushes rather than nylon for fine work, and a badger softener rather than a hog's hair brush, although nylon/sable-mix brushes are recommended for painting oil-based decorative motifs (i.e. those in eggshell or enamel paints). The same goes for safety. Do open the windows if there are toxic fumes, and wear protective clothing and goggles when using chemical paint strippers or burning off paint.

Another consideration to bear in mind is that there is absolutely no point launching straight into your chosen broken-colour technique if the surface is not sound. It must be smooth and sealed, not rusting, covered in grime, patched with cracked paint, or full of dents and holes.

This section shows in step-by-step detail how to design, cut and use your own stencils, and how to paint a mural. In addition, there are sequences on sponging—to create a soft, cloudy effect—and spattering—to create an exhilarating splash of contrasting colours. These are followed by sequences for the more unusual or difficult broken-colour techniques: stippling, combing and dragging, and ragging and rag-rolling. Follow the steps carefully if the technique is new to you, and do not hesitate in its application. Paint with confidence and you are more likely to be pleased with the results.

EQUIPMENT

Brushes

Decorators' brushes: pure bristle gives the best results. Available in 5 in (127 mm), 4 in (101 mm), 3 in (76 mm), 2 in (50 mm), 1 in (25 mm) and ½ in (12 mm) sizes.

Roller and tray: for applying paints of all kinds, apart from gloss, over a wide area, such as a wall, use lamb's wool for vinyl matt emulsion and textured surfaces; short-pile mohair sleeve for eggshell, vinyl silk or solid emulsion paint.

Fitch: an angled ½ in (12 mm) brush for painting angled recesses and mouldings.

Hog's hair brush or badger softener: for softening and blending colours in broken-colour techniques. The latter is more expensive, but is superior.

Stippling brush: a hard-bristled brush for stippling.

Varnish brushes: more bristles per square inch than decorators' brushes, they produce a mark-free finish. Available in 3 in (76 mm), 2 in (50 mm), 1 in (25 mm) and ½ in (12 mm) sizes.

Stencilling brush: short, stubby brush for dabbing paint on to stencils.

Artists' brushes: vary tremendously in quality: buy sable if possible for water-based paints, sable/nylon-mix for oil-based. Used for detail work, sizes No. 3 and No. 6 are the most useful.

Mylar: a transparent material custom-made for tracing and cutting out stencils: it can be used as many times as required.

Stencil paper: semi-transparent, waxed paper for cutting out stencils. Not hard-wearing, it is only suitable for stencils that will not be used often.

Stencil card: non-transparent, oiled card for cutting out stencils for longer-term use.

Water-based paints

N.B. Any paint you use in a baby's or child's room should be non-toxic and lead-free. Check by reading the outside of the paint tin before purchasing. Some paints are non-toxic and are specially recommended by manufacturers as being suitable for painting toys (and baby furniture)—especially enamel paints, which are also tough and hard-wearing. (see opposite under oil-based paints).

Matt or mid-sheen emulsions: ideal for creating broken-colour techniques on walls. Thin with water for a translucent effect. Not suitable for painting on woodwork, plastic, metal, tiles or glass. On a newly plastered wall, dilute the first coat with 25 per cent water to form an initial priming coat. Apply to other surfaces direct.

Artists' gouache: available in a wide range of opaque pigments that can be used for washes and stains. Mix with white household emulsion and prime as for matt or mid-sheen emulsions. Not suitable for painting on woodwork, plastic, metal, tiles or glass. Ready-mixed indelible gouache is also available that is not suitable for painting on metal only. Prime surface with universal primer first, but use direct on plastic and tiles.

Artists' acrylics: available in an excellent range of colours, but are pricey compared to emulsion paints. They are also quick-drying, which leaves little time to manipulate the paint. Can be used for lining and stencilling on walls and fabrics (excepting bedlinen). Thin with water for a translucent effect or use one of the acrylic media available to extend and change the texture of the paint without affecting the colour intensity. Can be used on all surfaces except wood, tiles and glass. Prime new plaster, and plastic with two coats of acrylic primer and dilute the first coat of paint with 25 per cent water. Prime old plaster with two coats of acrylic gesso primer. Prime metal with relevant metal primer. There are also acrylic-based paints available specially formulated for stencilling.

Poster colours: crude powder colours that are not very concentrated, so make subtle tones when mixed with a water-based paint, such as white household emulsion. Prime as for matt or mid-sheen emulsions. Not suitable for plastic, metal, tiles or glass.

Artists' powder pigments: dissolve less easily in water than poster colours, but make excellent washes. Mix with white household emulsion (it should be stirred in extremely thoroughly) and prime as for matt or mid-sheen emulsions. Not suitable for painting on plastic, metal, tiles or glass.

Water-based glazes

A matt or mid-sheen emulsion glaze or wash can be prepared by thinning it with as many as eight parts water, to produce a soft, subtle finish.

Rather than buying ready-coloured retail paint for water-based glazes, you can mix your own by adding artists' gouache colours (available from artists' suppliers) to white emulsion. Although more expensive, this will provide a superior finish.

Oil-based paints and finishes

NB Never use oil-based paints on walls plastered less than twelve months earlier, or on polystyrene tiles, as this creates a fire hazard.

Flat-oil paint: ideal for use on all interior surfaces apart from plastic, tiles and glass. Do not apply to newly plastered walls: wait twelve months and then apply alkali-resistant primer first. Primer is not needed on old painted plastered walls. Used on top of the primer or ground coat to provide a high-quality, matt-finish top coat: use two thin top coats (dilute with white spirit) rather than one thick one.

Eggshell: for use on walls (although not on new plaster—see flat-oil paint) and woodwork, it provides a soft, mid-sheen finish. Prime plaster—which should be more than twelve months old—with alkali-resistant primer unless already painted, in which case no primer is needed. Coat wood with primer and proprietary undercoat before painting. Can be used as a ground coat or decorative top coat. If using as a wash, thin by adding up to eight parts white spirit. Not suitable for use on plastic, tiles or glass.

Gloss: provides a shiny top coat. Used mainly for wood; if painting new plaster, wait twelve months and apply alkali-resistant primer first. Painting walls with gloss is not recommended, however. Old painted plaster will need proprietary undercoat instead and wood will need a proprietary undercoat as well. Use sparingly, perhaps to make a feature of a tubular frame. Not suitable for use on tiles or glass.

Artists' oils: used for tinting oil-based paints such as white undercoat, eggshell paint and scumble glaze (see entries for priming instructions). They offer a sophisticated colour range and are slow-drying. Not suitable for use on plastic, tiles or glass.

Enamel paints: produced by Humbrol in the UK and the US, these non-toxic paints are ideal for painting children's toys and furniture, as well as glass, metal and ceramics. Dilute with regulation standard white spirit; do not overcoat with clear lacquer or varnish.

Japan paint: fast-drying, thin paint ideal for stencilling on wood, metal, glass, ceramics and plastics. Prime walls and wood in the same way as for scumble glaze.

Spray paints: ideal for use on walls, roller blinds, metal surfaces and unwashable fabrics such as floor coverings. Particularly effective for stencilling. Do not use on newly plastered walls, and prime old painted plaster with acrylic matt emulsion.

Stencil crayons: a solid form of oil-based paint, they are suitable for most surfaces, although should not be used on newly plastered walls. Prime surfaces in the same way as for flat-oil paint.

Signwriters' paints: of thick consistency, these are suitable for painting large areas, such as floors, or on metal surfaces, plastic, tiles and glass. Prime wood with acrylic primer, metal with relevant metal primer. Apply direct to plastic, tiles and glass. Do not use on wall surfaces or paper.

Hammerite paint: this is a tough, durable paint that dries to give a hammered metal finish. Suitable for all surfaces (except aluminium, galvanized steel or zinc-sprayed surfaces, which need to be primed first), as long as they are oil-, grease- and rust-free. Paint directly on to the surface, applying a thick coat (the equivalent of four coats of ordinary paint) liberally and quickly. Do not add thinners of any kind. The first coat will dry in 15 minutes; if you want to apply a second coat, do so within four hours of the first. Note that it is not compatible with spirit-based paints. Keep windows open when painting and wear gloves and preferably goggles too. Highly flammable.

Wood stains: appropriate for wood in good condition, these add a translucent colour, while allowing the grain of the wood to show through.

Flat or eggshell, wax-free varnish: a specialized varnish suitable for protecting woodwork. Unlike polyurethane varnish, it will not change the colour of the paint underneath (polyurethane varnish is not recommended for this reason). Produced by Craig and Rose in the UK.

Oil-based glazes

These glazes are the traditional media for broken-colour techniques.

Scumble glaze: an oil-based liquid (available from artists' suppliers) which becomes colourless when thinned in a ratio of 1 part scumble to 1 or 2 parts white spirit, depending on the consistency required. It is tinted to the required colour using artists' oils, and provides a high quality finish with a degree of transparency in the colour ideal for dragging techniques. Coat walls (plaster should be at least twelve months old) with sealer primer first and then with a ground coat of oil-based household paint. Coat wooden surfaces with acrylic primer first. Scumble glaze is not suitable for use on plastic, tiles or glass.

Thinned paint glaze: an undercoat or eggshell paint thinned with white spirit to achieve the required transparency of colour. However, it dries quicker than scumble glaze, and therefore can be more difficult to work – though adding one teaspoon of boiled linseed oil to about a pint (half a litre) of glaze will lengthen the drying time. Artists' oils can be added to produce the required colour.

Oil-based washes: made by thinning tinted, oil-based paint with up to 8 parts white spirit. Like water-based washes, they reveal just a subtle trace of colour when applied to a surface.

Mixing and tinting glazes

When tinting oil-based glazes and washes it is important to create a uniform colouring throughout the mix. To be sure of this use either of the following methods:

1 Put a level teaspoon of artists' oil into a clean container, and add a similar quantity of white spirit. Mix them thoroughly to create a uniformly creamy consistency.

2 Add a small quantity of scumble glaze to the mix, and again blend thoroughly.

3 Slowly add this mixture to the rest of the scumble glaze, stirring all the time, until the required colour is achieved.

4 The mixture can then be thinned in a ratio of up to 1 part scumble glaze to 1 or 2 parts white spirit, until you have achieved the desired degree of transparency. If you require greater opacity in the glaze, try adding a little white eggshell to the mix.

Alternatively, if you are preparing a glaze from undercoat or eggshell paint:

1 Place sufficient paint for the job in a clean container.

2 Mix the artists' pigment with a similar quantity of white spirit and slowly blend it into the paint, until you have created the right colour.

3 Then add white spirit in sufficient quantity to create the desired trans-

parency – a ratio of 1 part paint to 2 parts solvent is usually appropriate, but this can vary, depending on the degree of opacity that you require.

Finally, adopt a systematic approach to the preparation of paints and glazes. Follow the stipulated proportions, where indicated in the text, when mixing glazes for the various broken colour techniques. However, do experiment: create 'samples' of different mixes on spare pieces of paper, and keep a note of the quantities used so you can, if needs be, replicate them at a future date.

Fabric colours

Fabric paints: for use on cottons, man-made fabrics and silks, they are available in pearlized, fluorescent, transparent and opaque finishes, and come in small pots or 1 litre (about 1¾ pints) bottles. Dilute with water for colour-wash effects, and intermix colours to make new shades. For pastel tints, add colour to white, not the other way round.

If you are mixing your own colours, make sure you mix enough for the job – even professional artists find it difficult to get an exact colour match if another batch has to be mixed. Any paint left over can be stored in airtight jars and will keep for some time.

Check the consistency of the paint too. If it is too thin, the paint will bleed into the fabric. If it is too thick, it will leave the fabric stiff. Remember to leave the fabric paint to dry before applying a second coat, and keep the fabric flat until the design is completed and dry.

Fabric pens: suitable for use on any fabric, these felt-tip pens are particularly useful for drawing lines and outlines as well as small details.

Fabric crayons: suitable for any fabric, these are ideal for use by children and the effect on fabric is similar to that on paper.

Heat-expanding, or puffy paint: with its thick, rubber-like appearance, this paint can be used on any fabric (even leather and suede) apart from silk.

Silk paints: for use only on silks, these paints have a translucent quality that can be increased by thinning with water. Intermix to create new colours.

Transfer paints: for man-made fabrics only, although can be painted on mixtures, such as polyester cotton, but the effect can be dull, as the colours will come out rather pale. Paint the design on to paper first and then transfer to the fabric by ironing the back of the paper, using a medium-hot setting. Although the colours appear murky on paper, they look brilliant on the fabric (even fluorescent in some cases), and can be diluted with water to create paler tones, and intermixed to create new colours.

Transfer crayons: as before, for use on man-made fabrics only; draw the design on paper first and then transfer to the fabric by ironing the back of the paper. Once on the fabric they appear very bright.

Fabric dyes: for use on natural fabrics only to give a new lease of life to a faded or disliked piece.

Fixing fabrics

Most fabric colours require ironing to fix them (always check manufactuer's instructions) to ensure permanency. When the fabric has been painted, leave it flat to dry out completely. Then, cover the design with a clean piece of cloth and, using a medium-hot iron, iron it for a few minutes, pressing evenly and firmly. Be sure to protect the ironing board with something like old, clean sheeting. Once fixed, the fabric can be washed or dry-cleaned (see cleaning instructions below).

Fabric cleaning instructions

Most hand-painted or -printed fabrics can be washed by hand or in a machine, but always check the manufacturer's instructions first, and use a mild detergent and warm water.

Items such as screens and blinds which are non-washable can be kept clean by regularly vacuuming them. Hold the nozzle about an inch above the fabric.

Fabrics that have been dyed may also be washed in a machine or by hand, but these should always be washed separately as the colour may bleed.

Ceramic paints

'Cold' paints: applied on glazed surfaces, these paints will scratch off with wear, so are ideal only for purely decorative artefacts.

'On-glaze' paints: these must be applied thickly before 'firing-in' in a kiln, as the colours fade significantly during firing.

Wallpapers

Lining papers: used to provide a plain, smooth surface before covering with wallpaper or a paint finish.

Duplex papers: strong, layered but non-washable paper. Available in a wide range of printed designs.

Vinyl papers: highly durable, moisture-resistant wallpapers that can be scrubbed: ideal for children's rooms.

Textured vinyl papers: vinyl papers that have been treated to resemble fabrics. Easy to clean and durable, they provide an interesting surface.

General tools

Bowls, saucers and jars: for mixing and storing paints and glazes.

Paint tray: for storing the glaze when sponging.

Palette and dippers: for mixing small quantities of paint for detailed work.

Clean rags: for cleaning brushes.

Plastic goggles and rubber gloves: for the protection of eyes and hands when using chemical paint strippers.

White spirit: used as a thinning agent in oil-based washes and glazes. Use regulation standard white spirit only. Not recommended for cleaning brushes. A proprietary brush cleaner is the most effective medium for cleaning brushes properly.

Paper: for covering surfaces you do *not* want to paint, for blotting excess paint, and for placing between front and back of fabric to prevent paint from seeping through to other side.

Hairdrier: for drying off very wet areas of paint on fabric.

Iron and ironing board: for fixing painted design on fabrics: follow manufacturer's instructions.

Low-tack masking tape: for fixing stencils in position and masking off areas where paint is not required, and for securing stretched-out fabric that is about to be painted. Will not damage already painted areas.

Craft knife: for cutting stencils.

Materials for special paint finishes

Marine sponge: used for sponging. Buy only natural sponges and ones that are no larger than the size of your fist. Man-made sponges are not recommended for sponging as they produce an even, rather flat pattern.

Rags: chamois leather or lint-free cotton are best, or try old linen sheets.

Used for ragging and rag-rolling.

Combs: metal or home-made cardboard combs can be used for combing techniques.

Tools and materials for preparing surfaces

Sandpaper: for rubbing down wall and wooden surfaces prior to painting. Available in fine, medium and coarse grades. Use with a sanding block, which can be made out of cork, timber or an offcut of wood.

Wet-and-dry paper: for keying painted surfaces prior to repainting and for rubbing down between coats. Available in fine, medium and coarse grades.

Wire wool: for rubbing down and keying curved or moulded painted surfaces. Available in grades 3 (thickest) to 000.

Chemical paint stripper: for removing layers of paint and varnish. Spirit-based, so always wear protective goggles and gloves when using it.

Gas and electric paint strippers: for removing paint and varnish, although they tend to char or burn wood.

Spokeshaves and stripping knives: for scraping off unsound paint and lifting wallpaper.

Filling knife: for applying filler to cracks and holes.

Fillers: for filling dents and holes in plaster and wood prior to painting.

Primers: formulated to prepare a wide range of surfaces for the ground coat, unless using emulsion, in which case a primer is not required. Ensure that you use the right kind of primer for the surface and the type of paint you intend using for the ground coat.

Undercoats: used on top of primers to provide a non-porous background for the top coat.

PREPARING SURFACES

Before painting any surface you must make sure that it is sound, clean and dry. This means that you must first remove any partially peeling paint, crumbling plaster, distemper, old, torn wallpaper or polyurethane varnish.

Removing blistered or cracked paint from walls or woodwork

Scraping off

1. Run a knife or spatula along the surface behind the blistered paint, keeping it flat so as not to damage the plaster or wood.
2. Repeat on all such areas, and sand down the edges of each stripped spot, using medium-grade wet-and-dry paper so that there is no obvious dip, or even out with filler. Allow it to dry and rub down with fine sandpaper.

Using chemical strippers

If you cannot remove the paint by scraping off, you will have to use a chemical stripper or burn the paint off. Chemical strippers will not harm the wood or plaster (although they will harm your clothes) and are generally better for removing emulsion paints. You may have to apply several layers, and be prepared to wait anything from 15 minutes to eight hours before the paint softens.

1. Open the window to let out fumes, and wear rubber gloves and goggles.
2. Brush on layers of chemical stripper, until the surface bubbles up. Then leave.
3. When the paint is soft, scrape it off with a spatula or knife for flat areas and a shavehook for curved areas.
4. Wash down the surface with proprietary solvent.

Burning off

A less messy, swifter method of removing paint, especially if oil-based, is to burn it off, although you run the risk of scorching the wood. Never attempt to remove lacquer using heat.

1. Work slowly from the bottom of the area up, heating about 1 ft sq (304 mm sq) at a time.
2. Follow immediately behind with a flat scraper. Scrape with the grain if removing paint from wood.
3. Wash down the surface with solvent, then rinse clean.

Removing distemper and whitewash

Old, powdery distemper will 'bleed into' newly applied paint, so must be removed first.

1. Brush the surface with a large brush to remove loose flakes.
2. Wash the surface with warm water, scrubbing vigorously and thoroughly with a stiff brush.
3. Wash with a detergent solution. Then clean the surface with fresh water and swab down with a cloth.

Repairing old painted plaster

In removing paint, you may well make dents in the plaster, especially if it is old, in which case it may be crumbly in places. Before painting, you must make the surface smooth again.

1. Mix the powder filler and tint the colour you intend painting the surface, especially if it is a dark shade.
2. Spread the filler over the gouged area with a spatula so that it stands slightly proud of the surrounding area.
3. When dry, sand down, using very fine sandpaper to smooth the edges.

Preparing bare plaster

A newly plastered wall should be painted only with water-based paints. If you want to use oil-based paints you must wait twelve months before applying them. See paint guide (page 000) for appropriate primers.

Preparing a sound painted wall

If the paint on a wall is in good condition, wash it down with plenty of water and decorators' sugar soap. Rinse off thoroughly, allow to dry and then start work.

If the wall is covered with an old oil-based paint and you intend painting it with a water-based one, rub down the surface well with sandpaper and prime with a coat of emulsion. If the oil paint is new, it will have to be removed completely.

Preparing wallpapered walls

If the wallpaper is in good condition, wipe down or vacuum the wall area. If applying oil-based paints, apply a coat of glue size before the undercoat first. For water-thinned paints, simply apply the first coat diluted with 25 per cent water. It is not a good idea to apply a sophisticated broken-colour technique to old, patterned wallpaper. The new paint will cause the dye in the paper to 'bleed' into the paint, spoiling the whole effect. In addition, the seams in the paper will stand out when painted. Also, wallpapers treated to withstand condensation should not be painted on.

Removing wallpaper

1. Try removing the paper dry, using a broad knife. This may work with thick, embossed paper, or if the wall is

damp, in which case, get this seen to before redecorating. Work slowly from the bottom up.

2. If you are getting nowhere fast, you will have to wet the paper. Score the paper first with a wire brush, then brush on a solution of household detergent and very hot water, using a very broad brush, from the top of the wall down, several times. (NB Turn off the electricity at the mains if you are using this method near sockets and light switches.)

3. Scrape off the paper with a spatula or broad knife, in horizontal movements, starting from the top of the wall and working down.

4. If you find there are layers and layers of paper, it is probably best to use a steamer, which you can hire. Hold the steam plate to the paper for 30 seconds, always working from the bottom up.

5. Scrape the paper across and upwards with a broad spatula or knife to remove.

Priming the surface

1. After removing the paper, wash down the wall and leave to dry.

2. Sand down with fine-grade sandpaper and swab the dust off.

3. Apply the appropriate primer for the paint you want to use (see paint guide, pages 132–4).

Suitable paints: water-based paints are ideal, although oil-based paints are also appropriate (see paint guide, pages 132–4).

Preparing bare wood

1. Coat any knots, which can 'bleed' resin, making unpleasant stains in the wood, with knotting compound to seal. Alternatively, remove knots with a chisel which should then be filled.

2. Fill knot holes and cracks with plastic wood filler and leave to dry.

3. Once dry, sand down the filled areas with fine-grade sandpaper. You may have to apply more filler if it has sunk noticeably: use fine-grade filler in this case.

4. Seal the whole surface with a coat of primer appropriate to the type of paint you are using (see paint guide, pages 132–4).

Suitable paints: oil-based paints are ideal; enamel paint is useful for detail work; use water-based paints only for colourwashing.

Preparing painted wood

Painted wood in good condition is a perfect base for a new coat; simply sand it lightly to provide a key, then dust off and paint. If the old paint is in poor condition, strip it completely and start again.

Removing varnish and wax

If you do not wish to paint over a varnished and waxed surface, which is possible only with oil-based paints, remove using a chemical stripper and scraper in the same way as you would remove paint. Wash down thoroughly afterwards with warm, soapy water, and allow to dry before painting.

Preparing metal
Removing rust

Before painting a metal surface, you must remove any rust.

1. For lightly rusted metal, apply a chemical rust remover (wear thick gloves). Then wash down thoroughly.

2. For heavily rusted metal, you will have to use scrapers, knives, wire brushes, sandpaper and wire wool to abrade it away. Once again, wash the surface down thoroughly afterwards.

Priming and painting

1. Prime bare metal radiators with zinc chromate while still warm.

2. If already coated with sound enamel, or once primed, paint with an oil-based paint (a water-based paint will rust). Use flat-oil for the most efficient conduction of heat, and do not paint a dark colour, as it will fade more noticeably than a light one, although light and pastel colours will tend to yellow after a time.

Preparing glass

Use window cleaner or hot soapy water to remove grease and dirt from glass before painting with oil paints, enamel paints or special glass paints (see paint guide, pages 132–4). Remove all solvent before painting.

Preparing tiles

Remove old paint from tiles using a chemical stripper. Otherwise, simply wash down using a detergent to remove grease and dirt and leave to dry. Paint with ceramic or enamel paints or artists' indelible gouache (see paint guide, pages 132–4).

Preparing fabric

1. Remove the manufacturer's finish or dressing by washing or dry cleaning the fabric.

2. Iron out any creases and make sure the fabric is absolutely dry. Lay out flat on a slightly padded surface. If necessary hold the fabric taut using masking tape.

3. If both front and back are to be painted, separate the two layers with paper on polythene to prevent the paint from seeping through.

Suitable paints: there is a whole range of fabric paints available on the market (see paint guide, page 134).

STENCIL CUTTING

Stencilling offers a simple way to create a repeating pattern or picture on any surface without the need to do any freehand painting. Choose from the wide range of ready-cut stencils available from artists' suppliers or make your own, taking motifs from any number of

1 *It is a simple matter to copy a motif that appears elsewhere in the room, for example on the curtain, and adapt it to use as a stencil. Spread the curtain out flat and iron away any creases. Place a sheet of tracing paper on top of the pattern and fix it into position with low-tack masking tape. With a soft-lead pencil, trace the outlines of the pattern on to the tracing paper.*

2 *Remove the tracing paper and turn it upside-down on a flat surface. With a soft-lead pencil, trace over the reverse of the pattern a number of times.*

3 *Turn the tracing paper right-side up again and tape it to a sheet of paper. Go over the outline again, pressing hard, so that the motif is transferred to the paper below.*

   Remove the tracing paper and enlarge or reduce the transferred motif until it is the required size, using a photocopier with this facility (available in most high street copying shops).

4 *Fix the photocopied motif to a flat surface, using masking tape. Then make registration crosses either side of the pattern, using a pencil and ruler.*

5 *Tape a sheet of clear 100 microns thick Mylar (available from artists' suppliers) on top of the motif. Using a fine felt-tip pen, trace the registration marks and the outlines of the leaves on to the Mylar.*

6 *Remove the Mylar and tape another sheet on top of the motif. Trace the registration marks and the outlines of the smaller flowers, again using a fine felt-tip pen.*

scourcebooks or from patterns found on other fixtures and furnishings in the room. These can then be used to create decorative friezes around the wall, add interest to wooden floors, and embellish bedheads, wardrobe doors and many other items of furniture.

7

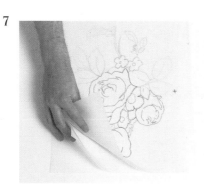

8

9

10

11

12

7 *Remove the Mylar and tape a third sheet into position. Then trace the registration marks and the outlines of the large flowers.*

8 *You have now traced the three elements of the pattern on to three separate sheets of Mylar. If you place the first two sheets on top of the third, lining up the registration marks, the pattern is reformed.*

Blocking-in and bridging:

9 *On each sheet of Mylar draw in the 'bridges' on each part of the pattern with a fine felt-tip pen to break up the pattern into its component parts, giving the finished design the traditonal 'stencilled' look and strengthening the Mylar once the stencil has been cut. Keep the bridges in proportion and follow the curves of the individual pieces so that their shapes are emphasized.*

10 *Thicken the inner edges of the outlines on all three sheets of Mylar with a felt-tip pen to 'block-in'.*

Cutting the stencil

11 *Position one of the sheets on a cutting board. Hold the blade of a scalpel or craft knife vertically over the pattern, and then cut along the inner edges of the blocked-in outlines. Cut smoothly and steadily, and remember not to cut out the bridges.*

12 *When cutting around curves, move the Mylar around the knife rather than the other way around. This will ensure that you cut a steady curve. Repeat the process with the other two sheets.*

STENCIL PAINTING

Traditionally, a stencil is painted using a stubby stencilling brush, using a dabbing or pouncing motion, producing a slightly 'orange peel' finish. Other methods you might like to consider include sponging (see page 142), ragging (see page 148) or stippling (see page 146). If the

1

2

3

4

5

6

1 *Place the three sheets of Mylar on top of each other on the cutting board, line up the registration marks exactly and fix the sheets in position with low-tack masking tape. With the tip of the knife, make a small hole in the sheets, in the centre of the registration marks.*
2 *Tape the sheet with the leaf outlines to the surface to be decorated, using low-tack masking tape. With a soft pencil, make dots through the registration holes on to the surface.*

3 *To provide a good key for the paint, lightly abrade the surface with a small piece of medium grade sandpaper through the gaps in the Mylar. Remove any fine dust with a small, soft paintbrush.*
4 *Mix up three matt or mid-sheen artists' acrylic glazes – green, lilac and red were used here. Do not thin the paints to more than the consistency of single cream or they will seep below the surface of the stencil. Then test the colours on a spare piece of paper.*

5 *Dip the stencil brush in the green glaze and dab off the excess on a piece of paper; the brush should look almost dry. Working from the edges of the outline towards the centre, dab or pounce the brush on the surface.*
6 *If desired, at this stage a little black can be added to the green glaze and applied to sections of the leaves to create areas of shading.*

motif is made up of several stencils, wait for the first colour to dry before applying any of the others; if the motif is repeated, complete one line with the first colour, allow it to dry, and then return to the beginning and apply the next colour.

7

8

9

10

11

7 *When you have finished, carefully remove the masking tape and slowly peel off the Mylar. Wipe any paint from the surface of the Mylar with a clean cloth if you intend to use the stencil again.*

8 *When the green glaze is dry, tape the sheet with the small flower stencils in position. Carefully line up the registration marks on the surface with the holes in the sheet. Repeat the sanding and painting process from steps 3 to 7.*

9 *When the lilac glaze is dry, tape the large flower stencil in position. Once again, carefully line up the registration marks on the surface with the holes in the sheet, sand the surface to be painted, and apply the red glaze in the usual way, again following steps 3 to 7.*

10 *Carefully peel back the last sheet of Mylar. If you discover any patchy areas, these can be touched up with a small stencilling brush.*

11 *When the paint is dry, an optional step is to apply one or two coats of flat or eggshell, wax-free varnish to wooden surfaces.*

SPONGING

Suitable for walls, furniture and fabrics, sponging is an easy technique to master. The finished result will vary with the paint used: emulsion gives a delicate, cloudy mottled effect, whereas oil-based paint gives a more sharply defined texture.

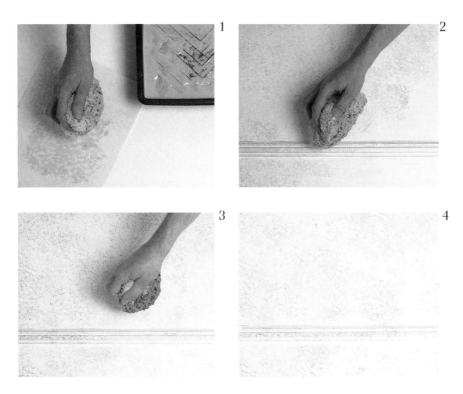

1 *Take a marine sponge (avoid synthetic sponges, which will produce a somewhat contrived uniform finish) and dip it in water or white-spirit depending on the medium being used and then wring it out. Mix up a water-based or oil-based glaze in the colour of your choice (see pages 132–4) and pour it into a flat paint tray. Dip the sponge lightly in the glaze, and dab any excess on the side of the container. Then test both the colour and the print on a spare piece of paper.*

2 *Starting from the top, dab the sponge on the previously prepared emulsion or eggshell ground coat. Keep the prints even and broadly spaced, and change the position of the sponge in your hand to ensure that you achieve a slightly irregular pattern over the entire surface. Each time you have to reload the sponge with glaze, dab off the excess on paper until the impression is clearly defined. Clean the sponge regularly in water or white spirit to prevent it from becoming clogged up with paint.*

3 *Allow the first glaze to dry, then mix up another water- or oil-based glaze, tinted with a second – preferably lighter – colour. Starting from the top again, sponge on top of the first coat and fill in the gaps. For a softer, more blurred effect, sponge the second glaze into the still wet first glaze.*

4 *When the final glaze is dry, protect wooden surfaces decorated in this way with two coats of flat or eggshell, wax-free varnish.*

DRAGGING

Dragging is a simple technique which entails running a dragging brush through a wet glaze to reveal some of the complementary or contrasting ground coat beneath. The result is a soft, fabric-like appearance ideal for walls and furniture.

1 *Prepare the surface carefully (see pages 136–7), and cover with an oil-based ground coat such as eggshell. Mix up a thinned eggshell or scumble glaze, or tint it with artists' oils in the colour of your choice (see pages 133–4). Do not over thin the paint.*
2 *Working from top to bottom, apply the glaze in a band no more than 2 ft (60 cm) wide. Brush on an even film that is sufficiently fine not to run.*
3 *Again beginning from the top, drag the underside of the dragging brush or a hog's hair softener through the wet glaze. If possible, use one continuous*

stroke from top to bottom. If you are painting a wall, to make sure each stroke is truly vertical, hang a plumb-line and follow that down. At the bottom of the wall, lighten your stroke to minimize the build up of glaze.
4 *Using a clean rag, wipe the glaze off the brush after every stroke so that each one is clearly defined. Overlap the next band slightly with the first, but do this before the glaze in the last band has become tacky, otherwise where the two overlap only the first layer of tinted glaze will be revealed, not the undercoat.*

5 *Allow the glaze to dry, then apply two coats of flat or eggshell, wax-free varnish to protect wooden surfaces.*
6 *An optional step, before varnishing, is to allow the dragged surface to dry, then apply a second glaze tinted either the same or a slightly different shade of the same colour. For a silk-like appearance, drag the brush through the glaze in the same direction as before, or to create the appearance of a weaved fabric, drag in the opposite direction.*

COMBING

Combing produces a starker, more stylized effect than dragging. It can look overwhelming on walls, but is very effective on floors and smaller pieces of furniture. Purchase combs from artists' or decorators' suppliers, or use pieces of plastic or card to make your own.

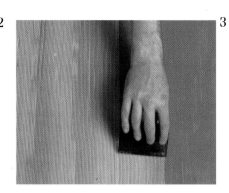

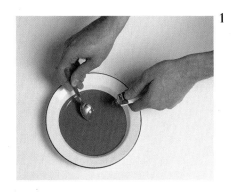

1 *Prepare the surface carefully (see pages 136–7) and cover with an oil-based ground coat such as eggshell. Mix up a thinned eggshell or scumble glaze, or tint it with artists' oils in the colour of your choice (see pages 133–4). Do not over thin the paint or it will dry too quickly.*

2 *Working from top to bottom, apply the glaze to the surface in a band no more than 2 ft (60 cm) wide. Brush on an even film that is sufficiently fine not to run.*

3 *Again beginning from the top, pull the comb through the wet glaze. If possible, use one continuous stroke from top to bottom.*

4 *Using a clean rag, wipe the excess glaze off the comb after every stroke so that each one is clearly defined.*

Do not allow the glaze to become tacky before applying and combing the next band, otherwise where the two overlap slightly only the previous layer of tinted glaze will be revealed, not the ground coat.

5 *Allow the glaze to dry, then apply two coats of flat or eggshell, wax-free varnish to protect wooden surfaces. If you are combing the floor, apply at least three coats of varnish to withstand heavy treatment.*

6 *An optional step (before varnishing) is to create a mottled finish particularly suited to woodwork. Pull the comb through the already combed and still wet glaze, at an angle of about 30 degrees to the first combed lines. Or create a woven effect by pulling the comb through the still wet glaze at right-angles to the first combed lines.*

SPATTERING

Though a somewhat messy technique, spattering creates a dramatic, crudely sprayed effect. Make sure that the paint is mixed to the consistency of milk – any thinner and the droplets will run – and avoid pastel colours as they tend to merge together and the effect is lost.

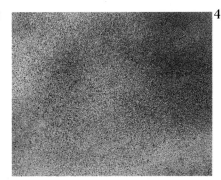

1 *Mix up two or three water- or oil-based glazes (see pages 132–4) in the proportions one part glaze to two or three parts white spirit or water. Apply an emulsion or eggshell ground coat to the surface to be spattered and allow to dry.*

2 *Charge a brush with squared-off bristles – a scrubbing brush or a stencilling brush are both ideal – with the first glaze. Be careful not to overload it or the droplets will appear too large on the surface. Stand about 6 to 9 in (15 to 25 cm) away from the surface and run a ruler or strip of* wood *in a steady movement in one direction across the bristles.*

3 *Allow the first glaze to dry, then apply the second glaze in the same way as the first, using a clean brush. Do not attempt to spatter the spray evenly over the whole surface: allow some of the ground coat to show through.*

4 *Once the second glaze is dry, protect the surface with two coats of flat or eggshell, wax-free varnish if it is wooden.*

STIPPLING

Stippling involves dabbing a flat-faced brush over a still wet glaze to reveal tiny pinpricks of the underlying ground. Use a stippling brush, an old hairbrush or even dimpled kitchen paper, shown here, which produces a soft, cloudy effect ideal for larger surfaces.

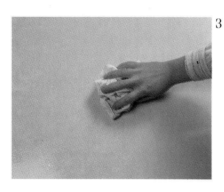

1 Mix up an oil- or water-based glaze tinted in the colour of your choice (see pages 132–4). Traditionally, a semi-transparent glaze is stippled over a lighter-coloured ground coat.

2 Using a standard decorators' brush, apply the glaze to a previously prepared emulsion or eggshell ground coat. If you are stippling a large area, such as a wall, apply the glaze in a series of vertical bands of about 2 ft (60 cm) wide, stippling each band before applying the next.

3 While the glaze is still wet, dab the crumpled piece of dimpled kitchen paper firmly in the glaze, avoiding the outside edge of the band. Be careful not to skid the paper over the surface, ruining the stippling effect. Discard the paper as soon as it becomes loaded with paint and bunch up a new sheet. Apply the next band of glaze while the first is still wet, overlapping the edge of the first band slightly and stippling over the join.

4 If you remove too much glaze from some areas, simply brush a thin film of glaze on to the kitchen paper and dab it on the appropriate section in the same way as sponging (see page 142). When the glaze is dry, apply two coats of flat or eggshell, wax-free varnish to protect wooden surfaces.

COLOURWASHING

Colourwashing involves brushing a highly thinned layer of paint over a light-coloured ground to provide a subtly shifting, luminous effect. Oil- or water-based paints can be used to varying effect on furniture and walls. Dry brushing, shown here, is a variation on this technique.

1

2

3

4

5

1 *Apply a white or pale-coloured emulsion or eggshell ground coat to the surface to be decorated, depending on whether the wash will be water- or oil-based.*

Mix up the wash in the colour of your choice. Dilute a standard or tinted matt emulsion glaze (see page 132) with one part paint to eight parts water, or an oil-based tinted glaze (see page, 133–4) with one part glaze to eight parts white spirit.

2 *Apply the wash thinly and evenly to the surface with a standard decorator's brush.*

3 *Then with a dry large decorators' brush, brush the paint quickly and vigorously over the surface, working from top to bottom or side to side on large areas. Allow the wash to dry.*

4 *To emphasize the effect, further layers of wash can be applied, allowing each to dry before applying the next, until you are happy with the depth of colour.*

Once dry, a coat or two of flat or eggshell, wax-free varnish should be applied to wooden surfaces for protection.

5 *For a slightly textured finish, and before applying varnish, apply the wash with an irregular, loose, slapping motion, brushing in all directions. Allow to dry, then apply a wash of the same colour on top in an even manner as described above. The textured layer will show through in a diffused and subtle way.*

RAGGING AND RAG-ROLLING

Ragging and rag-rolling can be achieved using almost any lint-free material. Ragging produces a sharply textured, bold-patterned finish best suited to walls, ceilings and cupboards. Rag-rolling should be used if you want a more cloudy, almost marble-like effect.

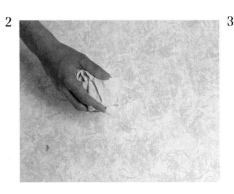

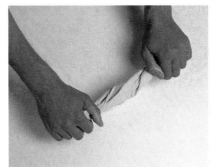

1 *Mix up an oil-based glaze in the colour of your choice (see pages 132–4), and pour it into a flat paint tray. A thinned eggshell glaze will give a softer finish than a tinted scumble glaze.*

2 **If you are ragging:** *take a semi-permeable rag, such as cotton cloth or chamois leather, and dip the bunched-up rag lightly in the glaze. Dab any excess on the side of the tray and on a spare piece of paper.*

Apply the glaze to the wall using a dabbing and rocking motion, continually re-bunching the rag to prevent the pattern from becoming too regular. Clean the rag regularly in white spirit to stop it drying out and becoming clogged with glaze or discard the rag and use a new one.

3 *Allow the first ragged glaze to dry, then, if you wish, rag a complementary or contrasting coloured glaze over the top of the first one.*

4 *When the glaze is dry, apply two coats of flat or eggshell, wax-free varnish to any wooden surfaces.*

5 **If you are rag-rolling:** *roll the rag into a tight sausage shape and roll it over the surface, again varying the direction and pressure to allow the ground coat to show through at random.*

6 *Clean or renew the rag frequently, and then allow the glaze to dry before applying two coats of flat or eggshell, wax-free varnish to protect wooden surfaces.*

PAINTING FLAT MURALS

Flat, decorative murals are especially suitable for children's rooms, and they are also relatively easy to paint, even if you are not particularly artistic. Because the compositions for flat murals are always representational – in other words, no attempt is made to place figures or objects in an illusory space, perspective and modelling are usually avoided and colours kept flat, with no gradations caused by lighting or aerial perspective – their success depends mainly on the use of outline, pattern and colour.

Choosing a site

If you don't want to paint a large-scale mural, the easiest way to limit its size is to create a simple frame in a basic shape, such as a square, rectangle, oval or circle. This could be used to represent, for example, a window or archway. Otherwise soften the frame by using, say, trailing leaves or flowers to break up the shape, or use an appropriate stencil (or stencils) to create a border.

The architecture of the room might also suggest suitable areas and subjects for a mural. For example, if the room is divided by an arch or an old double doorway, a mural painted round it provides a ready-made frame that won't take hours to paint. You could echo the shape by using long, elongated forms such as a Jack-and-the-Beanstalk type plant or a giraffe. Around or above a fireplace might be another suitable site, between two windows, or use the door as your basic canvas.

Once you have decided on a site, make a careful sketch of your design, especially if you are beginner, and fill it in with the colours you intend to use so that you have a good idea of how the mural will look at the end, and as a reference when you come to paint.

Right: this charming mural can be seen painted step-by-step on pages 151–3. Essentially a flat mural, some simple gradations of colour have been introduced to the basic shapes to suggest depth and form.

Transferring the design

There are two basic methods of transferring your design to the wall: squaring up and using a large-scale cartoon. Squaring up is a methodical technique that enables you to get over any inhibitions at being confronted with a blank wall. To do this, first draw a grid on top of your design with a pencil, consisting of approximately 1 in (2.5 cm) squares. Now with a soft pencil or charcoal, draw a grid at twice, three or more times the scale – depending on how large you want your mural to be – on the wall. You can also use low-tack masking tape to make up your wall grid. Use a plumb line and a spirit level to check that the rules are truly vertical and horizontal. You can now copy the outline square by square using a soft pencil or charcoal. Once transferred, your design is ready for painting.

The other method is to produce a design that is the actual size wanted for the wall. If you do not have a large enough piece of paper for your intended design, tape pieces together until you have the required size. Once your design has been completed, prick round the outlines with a sharp instrument, such as a pin, and then tape the paper in position on the wall. You can then mark through the holes with a pencil, or use cotton wool and charcoal powder to dust the holes to form an image. Carefully remove the paper, and join up the dots with a soft pencil to form an outline.

Before you start painting, you might prefer to partially rub out your pencil marks with a soft eraser in order to avoid any harsh pencil lines showing through your finished work, and make sure to dust off any excess charcoal if this has been used. Finally, before you commit paint to wall, go away and then come back and look at your design with a critical eye, and don't be afraid to adjust something if you feel it doesn't quite work.

Paints for murals

Household emulsions are quick drying and probably the cheapest paints you can buy. For smaller murals, many can now be bought in small tester pots that come in a reasonably wide range of colours. As far as durability is concerned, manufacturers quote a life expectancy of between three to six years, although emulsion paints will probably last longer if not exposed to damp or condensation. They can be used full strength or diluted with water to create thin washes of colour, and can also be mixed to produce new colours (but to be on the safe side, use the same brand when mixing). If you can't find or mix a colour you want in emulsion, you could try adding artists' acrylic paints, gouache or even artists' pigments to an emulsion base, such as white, to create the exact shade.

Artists' acrylics are not cheap, but they do come in a wonderful range of colours, as well as being durable and wipeable (ideal for a child's room!). They will also cover a variety of surfaces, including plaster, brick, plastic, metal and fabric, which gives them an attractive versatility. Acrylics can be used neat, diluted with water (to create translucent layers of glazed washes), or mixed with a number of specially prepared acrylic additives. These include retarder, which prevents acrylic paint from drying too fast so that it can be used more like an oil paint, and gloss, matt and gel media, which change the consistency of the paint and its final appearance.

Both household emulsions and artists' acrylics dry quickly, so if you make a mistake while painting, have a damp sponge or cloth to hand to wipe away any slips of the brush or splashes. Once the paint has dried, you can either remove it with a little diluted abrasive cleaning liquid on a soft cloth or it may be as simple to paint over any small problem areas.

Artists' oils are another option, but unless you have had some experience using oil paints and prefer them above all else, they are best avoided for the beginner, particularly as oils are slow drying and prone to yellowing if exposed to direct heat from radiators, water pipes and strong spotlights.

Supports for murals

Most people think of walls as the only surface on which to paint murals, but there are a number of other surfaces to be considered. Ceilings and shutters are obvious alternatives. A temporary mural can be painted on an old sheet, cheap cotton or canvas using vinyl matt emulsion (or fabric paints, but they are more expensive) and hung in place. Or marouflage canvas to a board such as hardboard for a movable mural. To do this, first iron the canvas with a cool iron to remove any creases, then cover the back of the canvas with an adhesive (use acrylic medium or undercoating if you are going to paint the mural with acrylic paints, and use glue size for oils). Then place the canvas over the board and smooth it into position using a roller (a rolling pin will do). Tuck over the edges and corners of the canvas and glue these to the back. For extra strength, you should cradle the board with strips of wood at the back (usually in the shape of a T-bar cross) to prevent warping.

A NURSERY MURAL

The step-by-step mural shown here can be seen completed on page 149. The artist chose to paint this small, narrow nursery with a background of pale blue sky on the walls and ceiling and applied a generous band of grass to the lower part of the wall, using soft pastel colours to keep the room as light and open looking as possible.

To paint the mural, the artist used 35 fl oz (1 litre) tins of vinyl matt emulsion in pale blue, white and pale green for the background, and then acrylic paints for the details from a palette of emerald green, dark chrome oxide green, raw umber, Turner's yellow, bronze yellow, raw sienna, mauve-blue, light magenta and mars black. These were mixed with the white emulsion paint as required. To apply the paints, she used two decorators' brushes, a 2-inch (5-cm) and 4-in (10-cm), and an assortment of artists' brushes, including a medium flat, medium filbert and small round.

The artist was used to painting murals, and painted directly on the wall with great speed and confidence. For those less skilled, sketch out your ideas on paper first, and when you are satisfied, transfer the various images to the wall using the squaring up method described on page 150, or simply trace them on if they are already the right size. You might also like to practise painting the various figures on some spare sheets of paper first: this will help to loosen up your brushwork and produce a more flowing, assured image.

Although a mural of this kind is one of the simplest you can paint, since figures are dotted over the wall in a fairly random manner, it is still important to link them up in some way, otherwise they may seem too disconnected. Sticking to one theme and treatment is the first step, but here, for example, the artist has also drawn the various characters together using the ribbon held by the bluebird. This might seem a simple device, yet it is just such touches that will help to create a more unified image.

1

2

1 Since the surface of this newly plastered wall was not uniformly smooth, the choice of background was an ideal one to cover up various minor imperfections. It was first painted with two coats of vinyl matt emulsion, the first coat diluted with 25 per cent water (oil-based paints should only be applied to plaster after twelve months), and when dry the sky and grass painted in. At the same time, the small chest of drawers and window frame were painted in the same green but in eggshell paint to provide a more cohesive look, especially important in such a small room.

The ceiling, which was also given a sky effect, was painted first. When painting such high areas, always make sure you have set up a stable work station. Ensure that step-ladders are firmly locked in place and level (never use old, wobbly ones). If you want to paint a large, high ceiling, it is safest to use is a scaffolding tower, which come in various heights and sizes from hire shops. Take frequent breaks when painting a ceiling.

2 Working from the top of the wall down, the artist used a medium-sized decorators' brush to apply unevenly sized patches of blue vinyl matt emulsion to the wall.

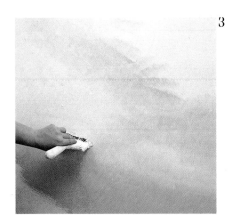

3

4

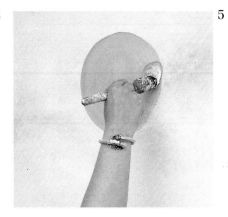

5

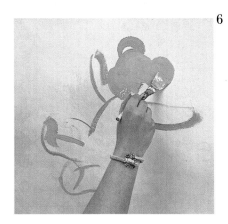

6

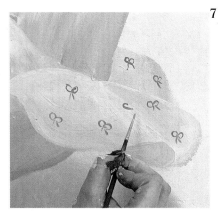

7

3 Then, in the left hand, the artist took a slightly larger decorators' brush and dipped it into the white emulsion and used a stippling motion (basically a quick stabbing action) to paint over and into the still wet blue paint. The artist also moved the brush with a twisting motion of the wrist in order to create uneven clouds.

Use old brushes for this technique as it causes the hairs to splay, and have a damp cloth to hand to mop up any drips.

A similar sky effect can be achieved using sponging (see page 142) or even rag-rolling (see page 148).

4 The grass was applied using a similar method to that of the sky, but the colours were more carefully merged together to create a smoother appearance. The radiator was also painted in this way in order to camouflage it as much as possible. Although vinyl matt emulsion was used here, this is not recommended by paint manufacturers. Ideally, special radiator paint should be used.

5 The artist used a mixture of light magenta, white emulsion and a little water for the balloon. Using the 2-inch (5-cm) decorators' brush, she applied its shape in confident, sweeping curves. The highlights, applied with dilute white emulsion paint, were then quickly worked in. For the beginner, it is probably easiest to draw such a simple shape on card first, then cut it out and trace round it to mark its position on the wall.

6 To create a more complex figure, like this bear, find a suitable image from a sourcebook, trace round it and transfer it to the wall using the squaring up method (see page 150). Then, as shown here, loosely describe the shape with fairly fluid paint. Here, the artist sketched in the outline of the bear and its overall colouring using a medium flat artists' brush and a mixture of bronze yellow, raw sienna and a dash of white.

7 The bear's frilly tutu was painted in with broad sweeps of the brush to suggest swirling material. Its curves are emphasized by using a darker pink for the underside (again, light magenta mixed with white), and a lighter pink for the top of the skirt.

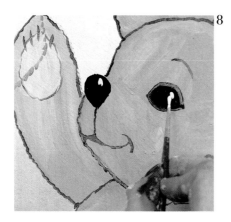

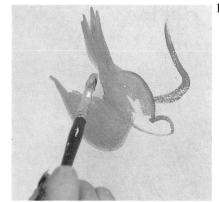

8 To fix the shape of the bear, the artist used a small round brush to apply an outline of raw umber to which a little black and white had been added. The same colour mix was used to form the bear's features, and at the same time the paws with their claw stitches were defined. The eye and nose were filled in with the black, and, finally, dots of pure white added to bring her expression to life.

9 The artist then turned her attention to the grass border. The leaves and stems of the foxglove were quickly worked in using a diluted mixture of dark chrome oxide green, emerald green and white. Using a medium filbert brush, she allowed the natural shape of the brush to form the rounded shapes of the flowers using light magenta mixed with white. More white was added to the mix to paint a lighter tint on top to give the shapes depth.

10 The bluebird was sketched in using diluted mauve-blue, and then filled in using a mixture of white emulsion and mauve-blue. Like the bear, the bird was also given an outline, in pure mauve-blue.

11 The all-important ribbon, which provides a much-needed link between the various figures in this mural, was painted in a mixture of Turner's yellow lightened with a little white emulsion, and applied with a flat artists' brush. Where the ribbon has raised curves, a little more white was added to the basic colour to give subtle highlights and to emphasize its twisting shape.

12 The delightful butterfly shown here was painted in using the palette of colours created for the rest of the mural. The wings are the same hue as the ribbon, its tiny body a combination of light magenta and white. A mixture of raw umber, mars black and white emulsion was used to paint in the other details, and the blue patches on the wing filled in with mauve-blue mixed with white.

As can be seen, this mural used very few colours, and this in itself has helped to bring all the disparate elements closer together. Its success also lies in the bold treatment of the various characters, which have nevertheless been executed with an attractive lightness of touch.

TROMPE L'OEIL

Trompe l'oeil literally means to deceive the eye. To paint such a mural, where the artist creates the illusion of three dimensions on a two-dimensional surface, requires considerable forethought and a clear understanding of composition, including scale, perspective, colour, light and shade. This is a vast subject, impossible to cover fully here, but a brief description of the various elements that must be considered in *trompe l'oeil* will at least give you an idea of what is involved, and perhaps the impetus to explore the subject further elsewhere.

Fitting the mural to the room

If you are a beginner, allow yourself plenty of time to design and paint a mural and start with something small. Analyse the room carefully first. Perhaps it has an outside wall, but without a window. If so, why not paint the illusion of one complete with an imagined view? Perhaps the room contains a fireplace with alcoves on either side. These would be ideal spots to create the illusion of tunnels, walkways, cupboards or half-open doors. If the mural is to be successful, it is crucial that the illusion be convincing in its position. The painted window or cupboard just might be real if situated in these places, whereas an open window painted on an inner wall would deceive no one, and probably create an uneasy atmosphere in the room.

Also try to link the mural to the rest of the room by painting, say, an illusionary window frame to match any existing ones in the room, or add curtains either side that feature the same design as, say, the bed cover. If

Below: a skillful example of a
nursery *trompe l'oeil*.

the door to the room is panelled, make the illusory one panelled too. If the room features an arch, frame the walkway with an arch. By framing the mural in a way that is consistent with the architecture of the room, the eye is more likely to accept the illusion as reality.

The viewpoint

At this stage, it is also a good idea to establish the main, or principal, viewpoint for your mural. Often this is from the doorway of the room, since the eye is usually happiest to accept what is initially presented to it, even though the mural will be seen from many angles once the viewer is in the room. Much depends on the site of the mural, however, but wherever the main viewpoint is, the design for the mural should be drawn with this in mind.

Determining the scale

Once you have decided how to incorporate the mural into the room without jolting the senses, consider the composition of the picture within the frame. Sketch out some designs on paper first to help you work out content and scale. Look carefully at photographs and paintings to see how they are structured. Also decide at what height the mural will be viewed from most. Once you have decided on your child's eye-level, you can establish the horizon line to which all the elements of the mural must relate. The horizon is usually most comfortably viewed at around eye-level. If the horizon appears much higher than your child's eye-level, then she or he will feel overpowered by the images, which will seem to dominate the room. If the horizon appears lower, then your child will feel as though he or she is looking

uncomfortably down on the images.

Once the position of the horizon has been established, everything else can be measured by it. The easiest way to do this is to draw a series of horizontal guidelines evenly spaced apart, starting at the base line of the design and finishing at the horizon. A figure, say, in the foreground will have its feet on the base line and its eyes level with the horizon. Use the horizontal guidelines to establish the scale of other figures in the mural design as they retreat into the distance, always remembering to keep their eyes level with the horizon, but reducing their size accordingly.

Establishing perspective

The next step is to decide how complicated you want the system of perspective to be. The simplest system is one-point perspective in which, if you stand or sit directly in front of the mural, all the elements in the mural appear to recede towards a central vanishing point on the horizon. More complicated, but also more realistic, is the two-point perspective system, in which the eye is led to vanishing points at either side of the horizon – for example, if a cube is drawn in two-point perspective, three planes, or sides, of the cube can be seen; in one-point perspective, only two planes – the front and top of the cube – can be seen.

When painting your mural, be careful not to give objects scaled to appear in the distance the same wealth of detail as those drawn large in the foreground, or you will ruin the sense of perspective completely. The eye simply will not believe that something featuring so much detail is sited a long way away, and the object will appear to jump into the foreground.

Colour and shadow

Use colour carefully in your composition to form links within the painting and with colour used elsewhere in the room: the eye will, for example, pick out all the red elements, blue elements, and so on, and link them together. Remember, too, the overall effect on the room: a blue cast to a painting will make the room seem cool, while a yellow cast will create the illusion of warmth and light.

To reinforce the illusion of perspective, it is important to incorporate shadow in your mural. If there is a natural source of light in the room, it is a good idea to extend it to the painting, so that the shadows fall in the same direction as those in the room at a particular time of day. Alternatively, you might want to make the light appear to come from the mural itself, in which case establish where the light source is coming from within the mural and cast shadows accordingly.

Avoid being too heavy-handed when painting shadows: build them up gradually and add the final touches and any highlights at the end. And do not treat them as separate blocks of grey – let the colour of the ground on which they fall modify them by building them up with layers of translucent glaze.

Vary the tones of colour on each element according to its position in relation to the supposed light source. Where the light falls directly on a surface, the spot that it hits should appear to be almost white, while the underside should be much darker.

And, finally, remember to stand back and view your painting regularly from the main viewpoint to make sure that everything is working together to create a truly believable, three-dimensional illusion.

*I*NDEX

ACKNOWLEDGEMENTS

The publishers would like to thank the following for their kind permission to reproduce the photographs in this book:

Camera Press 31, 33, 41 below, 87, 110, 116, 117 below; Condor PR 6; Dragons of Walton Street (Curzon PR) 15, 16 below, 40, 67, 108, 130, 154; Elizabeth Whiting Associates 12, 89, 91.

Special photography by John Hollingshead.

All other photographs from the Macdonald Orbis Archive.

Paint techniques on pages 26, 50–2 and 145–7 by Nessa Quinn; fabric designs on pages 70 and 74–7 by Kay Cunliffe of Kay Cunliffe Designs, 45 Kimberley Road, London N18 2DW.

The stencils featured on pages 20–9 were designed by Stewart Walton and appear in the *Jocasta Innes Nursery Stencils Collection* (Macdonald 1988)

Also special thanks to Nessa Quinn, Nessa Kearney and the Dragons Studio; to Sarah Duncan of Sarah Duncan Interiors, 4 Well Road, London NW3, for her help and advice; to Dominique Lubar of IPL Interiors; and to Mrs Kiaris, Carol Magowan, Emile Marsh, Mrs Massey, Annabel Merullo, Mrs Tamman, Sheila Volpe and Keith Watson for allowing us to photograph their homes.

Many thanks to all who helped so much with this book, especially to Jane Laing, Jennifer Jones, Bobbie Colgate-Stone and Judith More who did all the hard work! Also to Nessa Kearney, Nessa Quinn, Andrew Langhorn, Penny Thomas, Terry Skinner and Karen Murray, Dragons' studio artists. My thanks to all those who kindly allowed us to photograph their children's rooms.

Rosie Fisher